Academic Factors of Indian Society

Academic Factors of Indian Society

Edited by
Dr. G. VISVANATHAN
Professor, Department of Education,
Annamalai University, Tamil Nadu
and
Dr.S.K.PANNEER SELVAM
Assistant Professor, Department of Education
Bharathidasan University, Tamil Nadu

RANDOM PUBLICATIONS
NEW DELHI (INDIA)

Academic Factors of Indian Society

ISBN 978-93-5111-352-2

Published in 2014 in India by
RANDOM PUBLICATIONS
4376-A/4B, Gali Murari Lal, Ansari Road
New Delhi-110 002
Phone: +9111-43580356, 23289044
E-mail: randomexports@gmail.com; sales@randompublications.com; info@randompublications.com

Type Setting by : Shah Computer Graphics, Delhi-110094
Digitally Printed at : Replika Press Pvt. Ltd.

Contents

I
Reflection of the Society

I. Reflection of the Society

1

Introduction

"India lives in its villages" - Mahatma Gandhi.

Literally and from the social, economic and political perspectives the statement is valid even today.

"My idea of Village Swaraj is that it is a complete republic, independent of its neighbours for its own wants and yet interdependent for many others in which dependence is necessary.....It should have a reserve for its cattle, recreation and playground for adults and children....The village will maintain a village theatre, school and public hall. It will have its own waterworks ensuring clean water supply. This can be done through controlled wells or tanks" - Mahatma Gandhi.

Around 65% of the State's population is living in rural areas. People in rural areas should have the same quality of life as is enjoyed by people living in sub urban and urban areas. Further there are cascading effects of poverty, unemployment, poor and inadequate infrastructure in rural areas on urban centers causing slums and consequential social and economic tensions manifesting in economic deprivation and urban poverty.

Hence Rural Development which is concerned with economic growth and social justice, improvement in the living standard of the rural people by providing adequate and quality social services and minimum basic needs becomes essential. The present strategy of rural development mainly focuses on poverty alleviation, better livelihood opportunities, provision of basic amenities and infrastructure facilities through innovative programmes of wage and self-employment.

The above goals will be achieved by various programme support being implemented creating partnership with communities, non-governmental organizations, community based organizations, institutions, PRIs and industrial establishments, while the Department of Rural Development will provide logistic support both on technical and administrative side for programme implementation. Other aspects that will ultimately lead to transformation of rural life are also being emphasized simultaneously.

The prosperity of Tamil Nadu, like that of India, depends on the development of rural areas. As per the 2001 Census, Tamil Nadu's rural population was 3.62 crores, amounting to 58% of the total population. Ariyalur (88.6%), Villupuram (85.5%), Dharmapuri (84.9%), Pudukottai (84.6%), Krishnagiri (84.3%), Perambalur (83.9%), Tiruvannamalai (82.1%), Tiruvarur (79.8%) and Nagapattinam (77.8%) districts are predominantly rural in character. At the same time, Kanniyakumari (34.6%), Coimbatore (38.3%), the Nilgiris (41.8%), Theni (45.9%) and Madurai (48.3%) districts are relatively urban in character with less than 50 % of their population living in rural areas.

Firmly committed to reducing rural poverty in the semi-arid region of India, the Aga Khan Development Network (AKDN) and its partners are working to improve rural livelihoods in select and environmentally degraded areas in the states of Andhra Pradesh, Gujarat, Madhya Pradesh and Rajasthan. These are states characterized by erratic rainfall, depleting or contaminated groundwater, poor soil conditions and prone to natural calamities, primarily affecting agricultural incomes, still the mainstay of India's predominantly rural economy.

The profile of livelihoods in India, especially in these states shows that agriculture and animal husbandry still remain the main sources of livelihood for rural communities, though there is a significant shift to non-farm sectors such as mining and quarrying, construction and manufacturing during periods of drought.

The ultimate goal is for communities to have the confidence to make informed choices from a range of appropriate options that leads to sustainable and equitable development. AKDN's rural development programmes in India include community federations that have been promoted by the Aga Khan Rural Support Programme (India). Increasingly, these federations are taking over the roles and responsibilities of AKRSP (I) in promoting and strengthening community institutions at the village level. Support for watershed development activities by rural beneficiaries has given rise to savings amongst beneficiaries of 28.2 million rupees (US$ 622,222), increased amounts of water for drinking and irrigation, higher agricultural productivity, greater capability to cope with drought and lower payments to moneylenders. Community-based irrigation management, efficient water resource management and joint forest management approaches have been successfully piloted. A 1995-2000 impact study undertaken in certain areas showed beneficiaries' incomes increased between 40 and 80 percent, while expenditure on food increased by 85 percent. Female literacy levels rose by 10 percent while distress migration declined from 80 percent to 35 percent and distress migration declined from 150 to 90 days per year.

Socio-Economic Factors Affecting Rural Livelihoods

The poor have meager holdings or access to land, little or no capital and off-farm employment is seasonal. It is almost impossible for farmers to secure credit and loans needed to purchase agricultural inputs except at prohibitive rates from private moneylenders leading to risk-prone farming. Markets are under-developed or difficult to access. Extension services are few and far between, and development initiatives aimed specifically at their needs is sparse.

Few employment opportunities and low levels of education and skill result in low cash incomes. This in turn affects the ability to purchase basic needs (such as medicines, education for children, etc). Women and children in particular are the hardest hit especially when access to safe and adequate sources of water are low, resulting in high vulnerability in terms of health. Women are also more affected by underemployment.

The relevance of this is all too clear when one realises that 29 percent of India's population still lives below the poverty line, earning less than US$ 1 per day. A comparison with other countries in South Asia reveals that 33 percent of Pakistan's population is below the poverty line while it 34 percent for Bangladesh, 42 percent for Nepal and 25 percent for Sri Lanka.

Major components of AKDN's rural development programme include: institution building, social organisation, natural resource management (especially in the area of water management and water-use efficiency including in coastal areas), productive infrastructure development and human resource development (especially of women), enterprise promotion, increased agricultural productivity and credit and savings services.

Promoting Self-Reliance

A central strategy of the rural livelihoods approach is to put people at the centre of development, thereby increasing the effectiveness of development assistance and therefore improving performance in poverty reduction. Involving the poor results in local empowerment, which in turn leads to opportunities for local leadership, including that of women, to emerge.

These leaders play a critical role in bringing about and sustaining development and consequent social change such as pluralism, public participation and democratic principles. Village institutions form the basis of community organisation and function through 'Village Development Committees,' comprising of representatives of all communities in the village (including at least 30 percent women's representation). These Committees develop village development plans and work closely with the Panchayat (the lowest unit of the government that functions at the village level).

Other community organisations such as farmers' federations and women's self-help groups also facilitate the process of community driven development. These institutions work best if they have some independent means of sustaining themselves which is usually enabled by introducing them to micro-credit schemes.

For example, a women's federation in Bharuch district in Gujarat state recently accessed a loan-based scheme for animal husbandry. Likewise, federations of farmers groups have considerably reduced agriculture input costs (seeds, fertilizers and pesticides) through bulk purchases based on demand from member institutions, simultaneously ensuring the quality of inputs supplied.

These organisations have also contributed to improved cropping techniques, rational use of fertilizers and the adoption of appropriate low-cost technologies. Communities eventually go on to form "apex institutions" (federations of various community institutions) at the block (a unit of a district) and "taluka" (a unit of a block) level. These institutions also act as forums where regional issues are discussed and solutions formulated. These institutions also dialogue with the government and other agencies (including banks) to get access to and benefit from various schemes.

The federations also serve as agriculture extension agents, and transfer information from agriculture institutes related to cropping practices, thereby ensuring that information reaches farmers in remote areas. Collective marketing of agricultural produce, and enabling member institutions to sell their produce at the best price possible is another important activity.

Farmers' federations and the women's federations have also led social campaigns in the regions such as reducing unnecessary expenditure on social customs, promoting the education of girls, anti-liquor campaigns, and the promotion of organic farming. Mass awareness campaigns by women's groups in Surendranagar in Gujarat for example, have led to a reduction in wasteful and extravagant expenditure on weddings and on social customs such as 'funeral feasts.'

Skills Development

In addition to institution building, programme activities also include human resource development including skills development to build up the skills base of villagers, especially women.

For example, in the Net rang programme area of Bharuch district, women have been trained to repair and maintain hand-pumps. In another area women have been trained as masons.

Communities receive organisation and financial management training to support the effectiveness and sustainability of village-level institutions, and key resource people are provided with technical skills to plan, implement and maintain the development activities. The ultimate goal is for people in the participating communities to have the access, confidence and competence to make informed choices from a range of appropriate development options.

In 2001 alone, over 300 training programmes benefited almost 6000 villagers, 64 % of which were women. These were essentially to increase awareness about savings and credit programmes, provide exposure to 'model' villages and orient rural communities to the principles of natural resources management. In addition, over 50 NGOs and 400 government staff have also been trained in various participatory processes.

Creating Rural Assets

Institutional structures are created at the village level through which the rural poor can priorities their needs and decide how best to manage common resources.

Communities build personal and community capital through efficient management of their natural resource base such as water storage and enhanced water use efficiency, irrigation systems, soil conservation or forestry. These efforts include the construction of small scale infrastructure, such as check-dams, irrigation canals and water harvesting structures or agricultural storage facilities.

Over 400 structures have been created for harvesting and storage of rainwater that is directly lifted for irrigation, or recharging the groundwater aquifers for more rational extraction through wells. These have led to an additional 4000 hectares of irrigated croplands in the programme areas, which is being further expanded through the adoption of water saving devices such as drip irrigation and sprinklers.

Income growth is promoted by increasing agricultural productivity through improved farming methods such as using drip-irrigation, provision of better seeds, creation and improvement of markets, land development, micro-credit, increasing off-farm incomes and supporting enterprise development. Local capital is mobilized by promoting savings and developing financial services to enable broad access to credit. Programmes are designed to have a combined effect so as to create a critical mass of economic activities that raise living standards.

In Surendranagar area in Gujarat for example, it was found that a severely degraded natural environment would not allow rural communities to rear cattle and therefore the only viable option was to rear goats.

The rural development programme stepped in to help create a viable market for goat milk in the area and helped the community to get the government to set up a cheese making plant. In another water scare area, a women's federation lobbied with the government to buy them a water tanker which they now use to sell safe drinking water to local communities practically at their doorsteps and at fixed and mutually agree to prices. This has considerably reduced water scarcity in the area by providing households assured water supply and also saves women the time they earlier spent on collecting water.

Benefits and Impact on Quality of Life

Assets thus created often result in more than just increased income generation. AKDN's rural development programmes have benefited over 300,000 households in over 1,000 villages in western and central India since 1983. Development activities have ensured more water for drinking and irrigation, higher agricultural productivity and rural incomes (including household savings), greater resilience to droughts and the ability to manage the natural resource base better.

With over 10,000 households now accessing assured sources of safe drinking water, women have benefited significantly. Since they no longer have to walk long distances to collect water, the time saved can now be spent with family or education of their children. Alternatively they have more time for income generation activities.

Health improvements due to improved diets and access to safe drinking water also lead to a reduction in the costs of medicines and trips to the doctor. Similarly, the number of days of illness has been reduced by 50 percent (down to 15 days per year, as compared to about 30 days per year earlier).

Simultaneously, literacy levels have risen by 10 percent (8 percent in the case of women). Growing gender sensitivity and changing gender equations is also evident from a phenomenal 350 percent increase in the expenditure incurred on medicines for women. School attendance levels show an improvement, especially in the case of girls who now no longer have to accompany their mothers at dawn to collect water.

Impact studies conducted in some areas reveal an average increase of beneficiary incomes by about 60 percent, going up to 80 percent in some cases. More savings and increased access to credit reduces the dependence of the poor on local moneylenders. Even the landless benefit from increased demand for farm labour when improved agricultural practices results in two or three crops instead of just one every year, leading to, among other things, a reduction in migration. In 147 villages in four states, savings amongst beneficiaries was estimated to be approximately US$ 0.6 million (28 million rupees approximately).

As rural employment has improved, stress-migration levels have shown a marked reduction (down to 35 percent from 80 percent earlier). Even the duration of migration has reduced to 90 days per year (down from 150 days a year earlier).

Women's empowerment has also led to them participating in the local political process. In recent local village level elections in a programme area, 52 elected members (including 15 women) out of a total of 179 (approximately 30 percent) who were elected belonged to village institutions established by AKDN's rural development programmes.

Sustainability and Partnerships

Long-term commitment is the key to creating sustainable impact. Consequently rural development programmes in India have now run 20 years and helped create replicable models that can be quickly adapted to a variety of contexts; as well as long-term relationships with donor agencies and peer organisations for the mobilization of funds, human resources and expertise.

In terms of organizational elements, programmes are usually area-based programmes that serve a defined population, are implemented over a long time frame and at a significant scale and are characterised by comparatively thorough coverage of all of the population within their target area.

Ensuring sustainable impact requires consistent efforts over considerable time periods. In the case of rural development programmes, this has meant at least ten years of concerted efforts at the grassroots level before results and subsequent impact on the quality of life of the poor is visible for all to see.

Step taken by Government for Rural Development

The Government's policy and programmes have laid emphasis on poverty alleviation, generation of employment and income opportunities and provision of infrastructure and basic facilities to meet the needs of rural poor. For realizing these objectives, self-employment and wage employment programmes continued to pervade in one form or other.

As a measure to strengthen the grass root level democracy, the Government is constantly endeavouring to empower Panchayat Raj Institutions in terms of functions, powers and finance. Grama sabha, NGOs, Self-Help Groups and PRIs have been accorded adequate role to make participatory democracy meaningful and effective.

Aga Khan Rural Support Programme (India)

The Aga Khan Rural Support Programme (India), the rural development partner of the Aga Khan Foundation (AKF), is an internationally recognized, community-based, non-denominational, non-government development organisation, based in Gujarat. Since the early 1980s, it has focused on enhancing rural livelihoods through sustainable management and use of natural resources in degraded and resource poor regions of western and central India, often characterised by limited economic opportunities as well.

AKRSP (I) goes beyond merely addressing problems of food self-sufficiency and looks at the wider issue of poverty alleviation and improvements in the quality of life. Its programmes aim for broader, long-term economic and social development. The underlying philosophy is that rural economic development is best catalyzed and sustained through village-level institutions that are autonomous and transparent, contributing to democratic norms of behaviour and to the growth of civil society.

The "rural support programme" works in close partnership with local communities and the government to implement strategies that lead to

1. Income growth-by increasing agricultural productivity through improved farming methods, input supply, marketing, land development and management or by increasing on-farm and off-farm incomes and supporting micro-enterprise development;

2. Asset building-through community management of natural resources; water storage, irrigation infrastructure, soil conservation and forestry;
3. Mobilizing local capital - by promoting savings and developing financial services to enable access to credit on a sustainable basis;
4. Technical innovations - that on one hand help halt environmental degradation and on the other, help reduce the drudgery of poor people, particularly women, who can then utilise time saved more productively.
5. Human skills development - through training programmes that support the effectiveness and sustainability of village-level and community-led institutions by providing the management and technical skills needed to plan, implement and maintain local development activities;
6. Social Development - especially women's empowerment, equity and social justice and pluralism.

The ultimate goal is for communities to have the confidence and competence to make informed choices from a range of appropriate options for sustainable and equitable development. Particular success has been achieved in improving the management of micro watersheds and creating a variety of water harvesting structures in different agro-climatic regions.

Goals, Objectives and Strategy for Rural development

The prime goal of rural development is to improve the quality of life of the rural people by alleviating poverty through the instrument of self-employment and wage employment programmes, by providing community infrastructure facilities such as drinking water, electricity, road connectivity, health facilities, rural housing and education and promoting decentralization of powers to strengthen the Panchayat raj institutions. The Chief Minister's 15 Point Programme is a visionary programme which seeks to make Tamil Nadu the best State in the country by way of creating growth opportunities in rural areas and eradicating rural poverty. To achieve the above objectives.

The following priorities and thrust areas have been identified during the Tenth Five Year Plan period.

1. The goal is reduction of poverty from 21.12% in 1999- 2000 to 10% by 2006-07 and near elimination by 2012. Poverty reduction will be attempted
   (a) By organizing the rural masses into self-help groups and the Establishment of micro-enterprises, training, credit linkages, market Support, etc.
   (b) By substantial flow of investment in physical infrastructure like roads, Water supply and social infrastructure like health, education and Nutrition.
2. Special efforts for generation of adequate employment and creation of durable community assets to improve the rural people especially the small farmers, marginal farmers, rural artisans etc., through programmes like Sampoorna Grameen Rozgar Yojana (SGRY).
3. Decentralization of the process of planning by entrusting major role to the Panchayat raj bodies in the preparation of local level planning.
4. Improving the efficiency and capacity of the officials and elected local body representatives.
5. Providing all weather roads to all rural habitations having a population above 500 by 2004.
6. Strengthening of Grama Sabha the governing body of village assembly as an agency of social audit and to review the implementation of programmes.
7. Special efforts will be made to converge various schemes and programmes for accelerating the development process through special schemes like Village Self-sufficiency scheme etc.
8. Emphasis will be given for the maintenance of the assets created under various schemes.

Centrally Sponsored Schemes

Poverty Alleviation programmes

Swarnajayanthi Gram Swarozgar Yojana (SGSY)

The magnitude of poverty and disparities that existed between the various social groups necessitated planned state intervention to provide succour and relief particularly to the disadvantaged and marginalised groups such as SC/ST, women etc. Keeping this in view and having regard to the positive aspects as well as deficiencies, the earlier self employment programmes like TRYSEM, SITRA, GKY, DWCRA, IRDP and MWS were merged and a new self employment programme viz., SGSY was launched w.e.f. 1-4-1999.

SGSY Methodology

- o Group Approach
- o Organisation of rural masses into Self-help groups
- o Establishment of Micro enterprises
- o Training for improvement of skill & capacity building
- o Credit linkages
- o Market support
- o Provision of infrastructure facility

Sampoorna Grameen Rozgar Yojana (SGRY)

Creation of sustained employment opportunities for securing a minimum level of employment and income for the rural poor necessitated continuous need for special employment programmes. Keeping the above aim and to strengthen the need based infrastructure at the village level to boost the rural economy the erstwhile wage employment programmes JGSY and EAS were merged and a new scheme namely SGRY was launched from 15th August 2001.

Rural Housing

The aim of the State Government is to provide a dwelling for each family giving special emphasis to rural poor and deprived. The on going rural housing programmes will be given a new thrust.

Indira Awaas Yojana

With a view to meeting the housing needs of the rural poor, Indira Awaas Yojana (IAY) was launched in May 1985 as a sub scheme of Jawahar Rozgar Yojana. It is being implemented as an independent scheme since 1 January 1996.

Credit cum Subsidy Scheme

The Credit-cum-Subsidy Scheme has been conceived for rural households having an annual income up to Rs. 32,000/-. Subsidy up to Rs. 10,000/- and loan up to Rs. 40,000/- from commercial or co-op. banks is provided to eligible households for construction of houses. Out of the total outlay of Rs. 9.15 crores, 25% share of the State Government will be Rs. 2.29 crores. The physical target under the scheme will be 914.

Innovative Stream for Rural House and Habitat Development Scheme

This scheme intends to popularize low cost technology and usage of locally available materials in construction of buildings in rural areas.

Pradhan Mantri Gramodaya Yojana (PMGY) (Rural Shelter Component)

This scheme has been introduced by the Government of India under additional Central assistance for providing shelter in the rural areas to supplement the efforts in the sphere of rural housing considering the magnitude of the task.

Pradhan Manthri Gram Sadak Yojana (PMGSY)

The Pradhan Mantri Gram Sadak Yojana (PMGSY) is a Government of India Scheme introduced in the year 2000-2001 with the objective of providing road connectivity through good all weather roads to all unconnected rural habitations having population above 1000 by 2003 and all unconnected habitations having population of 500 and above by end of Tenth Plan period (2007).

Under this programme the approved works are grouped into packages costing more than Rs. 1 crore but less than Rs. 5 crores and executed through tender system. The guidelines stipulate that district master plans would be prepared.

A District Rural Road Plan is prepared for each district indicating the habitations in each block with the existing status of road connectivity. The scheme will be fully funded by the Government of India and an allocation of Rs. 750 crores has been proposed for the Tenth Plan, which will be shown under the chapter Rural Roads.

National Project on Biogas Development

Biogas Development programme aims to promote an eco-friendly Non conventional Energy Source with multiple benefits. The role of biogas as a major source of renewable energy has been recognized by the Government of India by including this scheme as an item in the 20 Point Programme. Prevention of deforestation, production of enriched manure and to improve sanitation and hygiene by linking sanitary toilets with biogas plants are the objectives of this rural energy programme.

This is a centrally sponsored programme with a subsidy component of Rs. 1800/- for general category and Rs. 2300/-for scheduled category and Rs. 3500/- for hilly areas. An amount of Rs. 500/-is provided in addition for installation and maintenance of the plant to the Turnkey agent. 10,000 bio-gas plants will be constructed during the Tenth Plan. The scheme is fully funded by the Government of India and Rs. 8.05 crores is provided for the Tenth Plan which will be directly released to the District Collectors.

Eleventh Finance Commission Grant

This grant is provided to Village Panchayats and Panchayat Unions for maintenance of civic services. Under Eleventh Finance Commission grant, a sum of Rs 186.45 crores for 2000-01 and 2001-02 was allocated. Out of this, Rs. 171.92 crores is provided to Village Panchayats and Panchayat Unions for maintenance of civic services and Rs. 14.53 crores for maintenance of accounts and audit and for development of database. An outlay of Rs. 659.47 crores has been proposed during the Tenth Plan period under this scheme.

Rashtriya Sam Vikas Yojana (RSVY)

During Tenth Plan a new scheme viz, Rashtriya Sam Vikas Yojana (RSVY)-Development and Reform Facility will be launched by Government of India. The prime objective of RSVY is to address the problems of pockets of high poverty, low growth, low agricultural productivity, unemployment and poor governance by putting in place programmes and policies, which would remove barriers to growth and accelerate the development process. Rural Development amount of Rs. 15 crores per year will be provided for implementation of various developmental programmes such as drought proofing (soil conservation, afforesation, social forestry, wasteland development and minor irrigation), agriculture, horticulture etc. infrastructure (road and power), social sector (health and education) and livelihood support (income generating activities such as handloom, information technology, agricultural processing etc.). Under the scheme 15% of the funds will be earmarked for maintenance of assets in health, education and veterinary sectors.

The main focus and strategy of the scheme will be on infrastructure development and income generation for under-privileged. The scheme will be implemented through people's participation, involvement of PRIs, NGOs and Self Help Groups at every stage including plan formulation, implementation and monitoring. Tiruvannamalai district has been selected on pilot basis for implementation of RSVY scheme. During Tenth Plan period the total amount of Rs. 225 crores is proposed under the scheme.

Various Rural Development Schemes Implemented by Central & State Government before NREGS

State Government Sponsored Schemes

(i) Anaithu Grama Anna Marumalarchi Thittam.

(ii) Member of Legislative Assembly Constituency Development Scheme (MLACDS).

(iii) Panchayat Union School Renovation Programme .

(iv) Namakku Naame Thittam.

(v) Periyar Ninaivu Samathuvapuram .

(vi) Rural Roads under NABARD - Rural Infrastructure Developement Fund (RIDF).

(vii) Twelfth Finance Commission Road works.

(viii) Programme for Comprehensive Development of Dharmapuri and Krishnagiri districts.

(ix) Rural Infrastructure Scheme.

(x) Mahalir Thittam by the Tamil Nadu Corporation for development of women Ltd. (TNCDW).

- o Mahalir Thittam
- o Credit rating and Linkage
- o Revolving Fund to Urban SHGs
- o Panchayat Level Federation (PLF)
- o Skill Training for Youth
- o Manimegalai Awards
- o Cultural Competitions
- o ID Cards to SHGs

Central Government Sponsored Schemes

(1) Indira Awaas Yojana (IAY)

- o New houses
- o Upgradation of kutcha houses

(2) Sampoorna Grameen Rozgar Yojana (SGRY)

(3) National Rural Employment Guarantee Scheme – Tamil Nadu

- o Objectives of the Scheme
- o Funding pattern
- o Priority of works
- o Special steps taken to ensure successful implementation of NREGS

(4) Swarnjayanthi Gram Swarozgar Yojana (SGSY)

(5) Total Sanitation Campaign (TSC)

- o Nirmal Gram Puraskar

(6) Member of Parliament Local Area Development Scheme (MPLADS)
(7) Pradhan Mantri Gram Sadak Yojana (PMGSY)
(8) National Project on Bio-gas Development
(9) Rajiv Gandhi Rehabilitation Package (RGRP) funded by Government of India
   - o Schemes which are implemented
   - o Provision of basic amenities in NGOs built sites
   - o Construction of houses and provision of basic amenities in NGOs backed out sites
   - o Reconstruction of vulnerable houses

A History of Programmes under NREGA

India has three decades of experience in implementing employment generation programmes. The concept of creating employment in public works is not new: the Maharashtra model of rural employment has existed since the 1970s. The most critical difference now is that people's entitlement, by law, to employment, is mandated through NREGA for the entire country. Not much has changed in the form and substance of the public work programmes in the past 30-odd years, however. In many ways the NREGA is a replication of earlier schemes in letter and spirit, of course, with a legal guarantee. So past failures do haunt the NREGA.

The first set of programmes, the National Rural Employment Programme and the Rural Landless Employment Programme, began in the 1970s as clones of the Maharashtra EGS. In 1989, the Rajiv Gandhi government integrated the two schemes into one, revamped the schemes and decided delivery would occur through the panchayati raj institutions (village-level elected institutions).

Thus born the Jawahar Rozgar Yojana (JRY); but it was radically different. The bureaucratic machinery was bypassed; funds would be deposited in the accounts of each village institution responsible for planning development activities used to create employment creation, and overseeing implementation. The scheme began but it was never given a chance to succeed. In retrospect, JRY was perhaps an idea before its time (See Box: Rural wage employment programmes in India).

In 1990, when prime minister V P Singh ambushed the Rajiv Gandhi government over the Bofors gun scandal, the election call was a promise to 'guarantee' Maharashtra-type employment for all. Instead the subsequent, Narasimha Rao-led, government diluted what existed. By 1993, JRY received little political leadership or attention. It was agreed (from largely anecdotal and some official reports) that the scheme, controlled by people's representatives, was leading to increased corruption and even greater inefficiency in delivery. Therefore, it needed to be re-vamped.

In 1993, the Employment Assurance Scheme (EAS) was launched. Now, half the allocated funds for rural employment would be channelised through the bureaucracy, not the panchayati raj institutions. The big brother was back in business, to the tune of roughly Rs 2,000 crore each year.

In April 2002 another re-naming took place. This times the two schemes — JRY and EAS — were merged to create the Sampoorna Grameen Rozgar Yogana (SGRY). Its spending, too, was divided between the panchayati raj institutions and the administration. Incidentally, in the National Democratic Alliance period the name of JRY had been changed into the Jawahar Gram Samridhi Yogana (JGSY). A component of SGRY provided food grain to calamity-stricken states for relief work. Now the cost increased to about Rs 4,000 crore per year.

Then came the semi-final reincarnation. In late 2004, the National Food for Work Programme (NFWP) WAS launched, targeting 150 backward districts. These districts were identified through a task force set up by the ministry of rural development, which used three variables to compute 'backwardness' — agricultural productivity per worker, agricultural wage rate and the scheduled caste and schedule tribe population in the district. This programme was to be implemented through the district administration and a menu of "labourintensive projects" would be prepared, to be undertaken over a five-year period. In the 2005-06 budgets, the allocation was enhanced. NFWP got Rs 6,000 crore in Addition to the SGRY's Rs 4,000 crore. The NFWP remains the programme design for the NREGA.

The final change came in December 2004, when the National Rural Employment Guarantee Bill was tabled in Parliament. The bill provided a guarantee of 100 days of unskilled manual work in a financial year to every poor household, in rural areas, whose adult members volunteered for work.

The first phase would cover 200 districts. But many believed the bill 'diluted' what the common minimum programme of the government had promised. The bill was referred to a parliamentary standing committee, which gave its report after two and a half sessions, called the legislation as "path-breaking" but observed that organisations and individuals who deposed before it were "almost unanimous" in objecting to several provisions.

National Rural Employment Guarantee Act (NREGA)

The Parliament enacted an Act No. 42 of 2005 called the National Rural Employment Guarantee Act. The Act provides a guarantee for rural employment to house holds whose adult members volunteer to do un-skilled manual work not less than 100 days of such work in a financial year in accordance with the scheme made under the Act

The scheme

Has been launched on February 2nd 2006 in 200 districts of the Country. In J&K State it has been introduced in the Districts of Kupwara, Poonch and Doda in the first instance. Is being extended to all other districts within 5 years in a phased manner. Is expected to enhance people's livelihood on sustained basis by developing economic and social infrastructure in rural areas. Is a direct attack on the causes of chronic poverty such as drought, deforestation and soil erosion.

The scheme is different from the earlier wage employment programmes in different ways

It provides legal guarantee of 100 days work to every rural house hold whose adult member volunteer to do un-skilled manual work. If an applicant is not provided employment within 15 days he / she shall be entitled to unemployment allowance. Rural Employment Guarantee Scheme is demand -driven instead of being supply-driven.

The focus of the scheme shall be on

- o Water conservation and water harvesting.
- o Drought proofing including afforest ration and tree plantation.
- o Irrigation canals including micro and minor irrigation works,
- o Provision of irrigation facilities to land owned by house holds belonging to SC/ST or to land of beneficiaries of land reforms or that of the beneficiaries under IAY.

Conditions for Guaranteed Rural Employment under the scheme

1. Registration to be made at the level of Gram Panchayat for issuance of job cards.
2. Duty of the Gram Panchayat to issue the job card after making such an enquiry as it may deem fit.
3. The registration for not less than 5 years and to be renewed from time to time.
4. Every job card holder entitled to apply for unskilled manual work under the scheme.
5. All registered persons belonging to a house hold entitled to employment in accordance with the scheme for as many days as each applicant may request, subject to a maximum of 100 days per house hold in a given financial year.
6. Such job to be provided within a period of 15 days of the receipt of an application or from the date he/she seeks work in case of advance application which ever is later.

Main features of Rural Employment Guarantee Scheme

1. The focus of the scheme shall be on the following works in their order of priority:

- o Water conservation and water harvesting.
- o Drought proofing (including afforest ration and tree plantation.
- o Irrigation canals including micro and minor irrigation works.
- o Provision of irrigation facility to land owned by house holds belonging to the scheduled Castes/Schedule Tribes or to land of beneficiaries of land reforms or that of the beneficiaries under the IAH of Govt.l India.
- o Renovation of traditional water bodies including desilting of tanks.
- o Land Development.
- o Flood control and protection works including drainage in water logged areas.
- o Rural connectivity to provide all weather access and
- o Any other work which may be notified by the Central Government in consultation with the State government.

2. Creation of durable assets and strengthening the livelihood resource base of the rural poor shall be an important object of the scheme.
3. The works taken up under the scheme shall be in rural areas.
4. The state council shall prepare a list of preferred works for different areas based on their ability to create durable assets.
5. The scheme shall be subject to appropriate arrangements as may be laid down by the State Government under the rules issued by it for proper maintenance of the public assets created under the scheme.
6. Under no circumstances shall the labourers be paid less than the wage rate, notified by the State Government.
7. When wages are directly linked with the quantity of work, the wages shall be paid according to the scheme of rates fixed by the state government for different types of work in every year, in consultation with the state council.
8. The schedule of rates of wages for unskilled labourers shall be so fixed that a person working for 7 hours would normally earn a wage equal to the wage rate.

9. The cost of material component of projects including the wages of the skilled and semi skilled workers taken up under the scheme shall not exceed 40% of the total project costs.
10. It shall be open to the programme officer and Gram Panchayat to direct any person who applied for employment under the scheme to do work of any type permissible under it.
11. The scheme shall not permit engaging any contractor for implementation of the projects under it.
12. As far as practicable, a task funded under the scheme shall be performed by using manual labourers and not machines.
13. Every scheme shall contain adequate provisions for ensuring transparency and accountability at all levels of implementation.
14. Provisions for regular inspection and supervision of works taken up under the scheme shall be made to ensure proper quality of work as well as to ensure that the total wages paid for the completion of the work is commensurate with the quality and quantity of work done.
15. The District Programme Coordinator, The Programme Officer and the Gram Panchayat implementing the scheme shall prepare annually a report containing the facts and figures and achievements relating to the implementation of the scheme within his or its jurisdiction and a copy of the same shall be made available to the public on demand and on payment of such free as may be specified in the scheme.
16. All accounts and records relating to the scheme shall be made available for public scrutiny and any person desirous of obtaining copy or relevant extracts there from may be provided such copies of extracts on demand and after paying such fee as may be specified in the scheme.
17. A copy of the muster rolls of each scheme or project under a scheme shall be made available in the office of the Gram Panchayat and Programme Officer for inspection by any person interested after paying such fee as may be specified in the scheme.

Conditions for Guaranteed Rural Employment under a Scheme and Minimum Entitlements of Labourers

1. The adult members of every household who-
   - o Reside in any rural areas; and
   - o Are willing to do unskilled manual work, may submit their names, age and the address of the household to the Gram Panchayat at the village level (hereafter in this Schedule referred to as the Gram Panchayat) in the jurisdiction of which they reside for registration of their household for issuance of a job card.
2. It shall be the duty of the Gram Panchayat to register the household, after making such enquiry as it deems fit and issue a job card containing such details of adult members' of the household affixing their photographs, as may be specified by the State Government in the Scheme.
3. The registration made under paragraph 2 shall be for such period as may be lapidate Scheme, but in any case not less than five years, and may be renewed from time to time.
4. Every adult member of a registered household whose name appears in the job card shall is entitled to apply for unskilled manual work under the Scheme.
5. All registered persons belonging to a household shall be entitled to employment in accordance with the Scheme made under the provisions of this Act, for ash any days as each applicant may request, subject to a maximum of one hundred days per household in a given financial year.
6. The Programme Officer shall ensure that every applicant referred to in paragraph 5 shall be provided unskilled manual work in accordance with the provisions of the Scheme within fifteen days of receipt of an application or from the date he seeks work in case of advance application, whichever is later: Provided that priority shall be given to women in such a way that at least one-third of the beneficiaries shall be women who have registered and requested for work under this Act.
7. Applications for work must be for at least fourteen days of continuous work.

8. There shall be no limit on the number of days of employment for which a person may apply, or on the number of days of employment actually provided to him subject to the aggregate entitlement of the household.
9. Applications for work may be submitted in writing either to the Gram Panchayat or to the Programme Officer, as may be specified in the Scheme.
10. The Gram Panchayat and Programme Officer, as the case may be, shall be bound to accept valid applications and to issue a dated receipt to. The applicant. Group applications may also be submitted.
11. Applicants who are provided with work shall be so intimated in writing, by means of a letter sent to him at the address given in the job card and by a public notice displayed at the office of the Panchayats at the district, intermediate or village level.
12. As far as possible, employment shall be provided within a radius of five kilometers of the village where the applicant resides at the time of applying.
13. A new work under the Scheme shall be commenced only if-
    - ✓ At least fifty labourers become available for such work; and
    - ✓ The labourers cannot be absorbed in the ongoing works: Provided that this condition shall not be applicable for new works, as determined by the State Government, in hilly areas and in respect of afforest ration.
14. In cases the employment is provided outside such radius, it must be provided within the Block, and the labourers shall be paid ten per cent. Of the wage rate as extra wages to meet additional transportation and living expenses.
15. A period of employment shall ordinarily be at least fourteen days continuously with not more than six days in a week.
16. In all cases where unemployment allowance is paid, or due to be paid, the Programme Officer shall inform the District Programme Coordinator in writing the reasons why it was

not possible for him to provide employment or cause to provide employment to the applicants.

17. The District Programme Coordinator shall, in his Annual Report to the State Council, explain as to why employment could not be provided in cases where payment of unemployment allowance is involved.
18. Provision shall be made in the Scheme for advance applications, that is, an application which may be submitted in advance of the date from which employment is sought.
19. Provision shall be made in the Scheme for submission of multiple applications by the same person provided that the corresponding periods for which employment is sought do not overlap.
20. The Gram Panchayat shall prepare and maintain or cause to be prepared and maintained such registers, vouchers and other documents in such form and in such manner as may be specified in the Scheme containing particulars of job cards and passbooks issued, name, age and address of the head of the household and the adult members of the household registered with the Gram Panchayat.
21. The Gram Panchayat shall send such list or lists of the names and addresses of households and their adult members registered with it and supply such other information to the concerned Programme Officer at such periods and in such form as may be specified in the Scheme.
22. A list of persons who are provided with the work shall be displayed on the notice board of the Gram Panchayat and at the office of the Programme Officer and at such other places as the Programme Officer may deem necessary and the list shall be open for inspection by the State Government and any person interested.
23. If the Gram Panchayat is satisfied at any time that a person has registered with it by furnishing false information, it may direct the Programme Officer to direct his name to be struck off from the register and direct the applicant to return the job card: Provided that no such action under this paragraph shall

be directed unless the applicant has been given an opportunity of being heard in the presence of two independent persons.

24. If any personal injury is caused to any person employed under the Scheme by accident arising out of and in the course of his employment, he shall be entitled to, free of charge, such medical treatment as is admissible under the Scheme.

25. Where hospitalization of the injured worker is necessary, the State Government shall arrange for such hospitalization including accommodation, treatment, medicines and payment of daily allowance not less than half of the wage rate required to be paid had the injured been engaged in the work.

26. If a person employed under a Scheme dies or becomes permanently disabled by accident arising out of and in the course of employment, he shall be paid by the implementing agency an ex gratia payment at the rate of twenty- five thousand rupees or such amount as may be notified by the Central Government, and the amount shall be paid to the legal he iris of the deceased or the disabled, as the case may be.

27. The facilities of safe drinking water, shade for children and periods of rest, first-aid box with adequate material for emergency treatment for minor injuries and other health hazards connected with the work being performed shall be provided at the work site.

28. In case the number of children below the age of six years accompanying the women working at any site is five or more, provisions shall be made to depute one of such women worker to look after such children.

29. The person deputed under paragraph 28 shall be paid wage rate.

30. In case the payment of wages is not made within the period specified under the Scheme, the labourers shall be entitled to receive payment of compensation as per the provisions of the Payment of Wages Act, 1936 (4 of 1936).

31. The wages under a Scheme may be paid either wholly in cash or in cash and kind provided that at least one- fourth of the wages shall be paid in cash only.

32. The State Government may prescribe that a portion of the wages in cash may be paid to the labourers on a daily basis during the period of employment.
33. If any personal injury is caused by accident to a child accompanying any person who is employed under a Scheme, such person shall be entitled to, free of charge, such medical treatment for the child as may be specified in the Scheme and in case of death or disablement, through an excreta payment as may be determined by the State Government.
34. In case of every employment under the Scheme, there shall be no discrimination solely on the ground of gender and the provisions of the Equal Remuneration Act, 1976 (25 of 1976), shall be complied with.

The National Rural Employment Guarantee Scheme (NREGS)

The National Rural Employment Guarantee Scheme has been launched in,more than150 most backward districts of the country, identified by the Planning Commission in consultation with the Ministry of Rural Development and the State Governments. This Programme was formerly known as National Food for Work Programmme.

Need

The existing resources in the SGRY were not sufficient to meet the requirement of additional wage employment in most backward districts. Moreover, it was felt that the additional resources should be channelised into some focus areas like water conservation and drought proofing which is the principal problem in some States and a major cause of backwardness of certain regions. Some areas are flood-prone and measures for flood control require special attention in these areas in a planned manner.

The States were finding difficult to provide State share of funds and therefore, a 100% Centrally Sponsored Scheme was proposed so that the investment in backward areas does not suffer because of lack of resources available with the States.

A need for the preparation of Perspective Plan under the NREGS was felt, to assess the work force/wage seekers available in the villages and to identify need based optimum infrastructure at the Panchayat Level for creation of a sound base, for self sustaining economy to remove poverty and bring this district at least on par with other developed areas of the state and country. The Perspective Plan aims at creation of need based optimum infrastructure at the Panchayat Level

During the preparation of Perspective Plan, National Rural Employment Guarntee Act 2006, came in to force. This plan has been transformed under the light of the said act, an act to provide, enhancement of livelihood security of the households in rural areas of the district by providing at least one hundred days of guaranteed wage employment in every financial year to every household whose adult members volunteer to do unskilled manual work.

NREGS in Ariyalur District

National Rural Employment Guarantee Scheme - Tamil Nadu

The National Rural Employment Guarantee Scheme was initially implemented in six notified (Phase I) districts viz. Cuddalore, Villupuram, Tiruvannamalai, Nagapattinam, Dindigul and Sivagangai districts from 2.2.06. In the second phase, it was extended to Thanjavur, Tiruvarur, Karur and Tirunelveli districts with effect from01.04.2007. From 01.04.2008 onwards, the Scheme has been extended to all the remaining 20 districts (Phase III) of Tamilnadu viz. 1. Ariyalur, 2. Dharmapuri, 3. Perambalur, 4. Pudukottai, 5. Ramanathapuram, 6. Namakkal, 7. Vellore, 8. Thoothu kudi, 9. Virudhunar 10. Salem, 11. Erode, 12. Tiruchirapalli, 13. Kancheepuram 14. Theni, 15. Tiruvallur, 16. Madurai, 17. Nilgiris, 18. Kanniyakumari, 19. Coimbatore and 20. Krishnagiri.

Objectives of the Scheme

The National Rural Employment Guarantee Act, 2005 (NREGA) guarantees 100 days of employment in a financial year to any rural household whose adult members are willing to do unskilled manual work. This Act is an important step towards the realization of the right to work. It is also expected to enhance people's livelihoods on a sustained basis, by developing the economic and social infrastructure in rural areas.

The Village Panchayat will issue job cards to every registered individual. Payment of the statutory minimum wage and equal wages for men and women are the notable features of the scheme.

Funding Pattern

The cost of the scheme is shared between the Centre and the State in the ratio of 90:10. The Central Government will bear the following costs:

- o The entire cost of wages for unskilled manual workers.
- o 75 percent of the cost of material and wages for skilled and semi-skilled workers.
- o Administrative expenses, which will include, inter alia, the salary and allowances of Programme Officers and their support staff and work site facilities.
- o Administrative expenses of the Central Employment Guarantee Council.

The State Government will bear the following costs

- o 25 percent of the cost of material and wages for skilled and semi-skilled workers.
- o Unemployment allowance payable in case the State Government cannot provide wage employment within 15 days of application.
- o Administrative expenses of the State Employment Guarantee Council.

Priority of works

Taking into account the field conditions in Tamil Nadu, the works are being taken up in Tamil Nadu in the following priority:

- o Formation of new ponds.
- o Renovation of existing Ponds, Kuttais, Kulams, Ooranies, and Temple tanks etc.
- o Desilting of channels.

- o Desilting and strengthening of bunds of irrigation tanks.
- o Formation of new roads.
- o Other water conservation/soil conservation measures/flood protection measures.

Special steps taken to ensure successful implementation of NREGS

On assumption of office in the month of May 2006, this Government noticed that the scheme had not taken off properly. This was evident from the fact that the expenditure made was only Rs. 3 crores and that works had been taken up only in 924 Village Panchayats out of a total of 3,830 Village Panchayats in the six districts.

This Government was quick to identify the issues and bottlenecks that were responsible for the poor progress in the implementation of the programme and came out with a series of initiatives to address those issues and to remove the implementation bottlenecks.

The following special steps were initiated to streamline and expedite the implementation of the scheme

1. A separate Rural Schedule of Rates was approved exclusively for this scheme in the G.O.Ms. No. 77, RD & PR (CGS-1) Department dated 14.07.2006, thereby removing a major hurdle in getting the statutory minimum wage of Rs.80 per day for seven hours of prescribed work. Rates for working on laterite rock, which is common in Sivaganga district, were added to the Schedule vide G.O M.S No 35 RD & PR Department dated 12.3.2007. The Rural Schedule of Rates under National Rural Employment Guarantee Scheme for the year 2007-08 was ordered in G.O.No.101 RD & PR (CGS-I) Department dated 13.06.2007.
2. A minimum of 30% registrations has been insisted upon in each Village Panchayat. The average percentage of registration in the Phase-I districts is over 65%. In the Phase-II districts, the average registration has crossed 50%, which indicates that there is widespread awareness about the scheme.

3. The existing formats of Job Cards and Nominal Muster Rolls have been revised to make these documents more transparent informative and difficult to manipulate in the process of scheme implementation.
4. Since the scheme requires intensive touring, the Government has sanctioned additional fuel of 50 litres per month for each of the vehicles in the Panchayat Unions. The Government have also sanctioned additional fuel of 75 litres for the vehicles of the Assistant Executive Engineers (RD) vide G.O.Ms.No.27 RD&PR (CGS-I) Department dated 20.02.2008.
5. Makkal Nala Paniyalars (MNPs) have also been made responsible for the implementation of the scheme at the field level.
6. Additional ministerial, technical and computer staff has been sanctioned at District, Division, Block and Village levels in order to ensure proper implementation and close supervision of the scheme.
7. Only 100% labour intensive works have been taken up in order to prevent the entry of contractors who are strictly banned as per the NREG Act.
8. Only bigger works not less than Rs. 3 lakhs in value have been taken up in order to ensure that i) adequate numbers of workers get sustained employment at a work site for at least 30 days, ii) the assets created are visible, durable and genuinely beneficial to the community, iii) resources are not wasted by being spread too thinly, iv) the works are monitored closely and leakages are minimised.
9. In order to ensure greater transparency and fair play, it has been ordered to disburse the wages to the workers in the presence of at least four members of the following committee:
   - o President of the Village Panchayat.
   - o Vice–President of the Village Panchayat
   - o Ward Member of the area where the work is executed
   - o An SC/ST Ward Member, if none of the persons in Sl.Nos. 1, 2 and 3 belongs to SC/ST Community.

- o Two animators of graded Self Help Groups.
- o A representative of the Panchayat Level federation.

10. A 25-member Tamil Nadu State Employment Guarantee council has been constituted vide the G.O Ms No. 117, RD & PR (CGS-I) Department, dated 14.09.2006 to monitor and review the implementation of the scheme. The first, second and third meetings of this council were held on 25.11.2006, 11.06.2007 and 03.03.2008 respectively.
11. In order to ensure efficient monitoring of the scheme through Management Information System (MIS), three computers and a printer have been sanctioned to each of the 141 block offices of Phase-I and II NREGS districts. In 2008-09, computers, printers and computer room facilities will also be provided for the block offices of Phase-III NREGS districts.
12. In order to ensure a total transparency in the implementation of the Scheme, the Government ordered for the conduct of Social Audit of the Scheme in all Village Panchayats of NREGS districts along with the conduct of Grama Sabha meeting on 15th August, 2nd October and 26th January in 2007-08. Likewise, the conduct of Social Audit of the scheme will be conducted along with Grama Sabha meetings in the year 2008-09 also. As a result of the concerted efforts taken by this Government, a sum of Rs.619 crores has been utilized and over 800 lakh mandays of employment have been generated up to 31.03.2008. About 82% of the work force comprises women and 56% are Scheduled Castes. A notable feature of the scheme is that it has had a buoyant effect on rural wages.

National Rural Employment Guarantee Scheme (NREGS)

(I) Central Government

- o Rural development ministry nodal ministry
- o Ensure fund flow
- o Set up employment guarantee council for advisory
- o Independent monitoring and evaluation

(II) State Government

- o Evolve regulations
- o Set up Employment Guarantee Council
- o Facilitating resource flow

(III) District Panchayat

- o Prepare district annual plan
- o Prepare five-year perspective plan based on village plans
- o Implement works (not mandatory)
- o District level coordination of activities

(IV) Block Panchayat

- o Coordinate block level plans
- o Identify possible works based on village plan
- o Design and implement works (not mandatory)
- o Monitoring

(V) Village Panchayat

- o Prepare village plan
- o Identify, design and implement 50% works
- o Set up local institutions to facilitate implementation
- o Evaluate and monitor implementation

2

Review of Literature

Review of literature is an important part of the research process. Studies related to the research problem have been reviewed and documented in this chapter. The present study focuses on the implementation of NREGS, Awareness on the programme and various other topics related to the scheme. The researcher could get only studies that were related in some ways or other with the key variables and such studies have been reviewed and classified under different related areas as follows.

1. Implementation of NREGS
2. Significance of NREGS
3. Awareness on NREGS.
4. Impact of NREGS.
5. Women and Child Care.
6. Social Audit.

Implementation of NREGS

Sharma and Bajpai (2006), Studied the implementation of NREGS in selected Districts of U.P. The government identified 22 districts as backward. For the implementation of NREGS but has increased 17 more districts later on. However the author has taken four districts namely Barabanki, Raebareli, Sitapur and Unnao for the Study. The objectives of the Study were as follows.

1. There is general awareness about the scheme among the villages.
2. The scheme is providing jobs to the application without hassles.
3. The beneficiaries and the village people appreciate the implementation of the scheme.
4. The project has potential to create job opportunities in the area and
5. To make suggestion for effective implementation of NREGS to benefit the poor people living in the rural areas.

The survey exercise was conducted by administering a structured questionnaire schedule on the beneficiaries of the scheme at the worksite in the 16 villages spread over four select districts on the basis of convenient sampling. He has selected two blocks from each district and two villages from each block on random basis. The sample at each village's worksite was 25. Thus 100 beneficiaries were interviewed making the total sample size of 400 beneficiaries.

The study of four districts identified most backward districts of Uttar Pradesh underscores the important role of panchayat Raj Institutions. It revealed the ground realities of the implementation of the scheme. The scheme has provided relief and succulence to poor village people. It was also found that the people were happy about getting the job opportunities in their own villages. However they want increase in wage and worksite facilities. But the participation of women has not been found encouraging. The author concludes that efforts to create quality awareness on massive scale can provide fillip to efficient and effective implementation of the NREGS.

Rao (2008), presents an overall view on the implementation of the NREGS scheme. In his report published in kurukshetra, June

2008. The author states that according to the latest figures employment provided to 3.08 households as against the demand by 3.10 households. A total of 121.64 crore person days have been created. This includes 32.89 crore person days of scheduled castes and 36.50 crore persondays of Schedule Tribes. Women constituted 51.24 crore persons days.

The author further states that the NREGS programme has strengthened the bargaining capacity of the workers in fixing the minimum wages. It also gave a big boost to the water conservation. Its implementation in some of the nexal – affected areas was very effective. It has helped in reducing the distress of migration of labourers from rural areas to the urban locations.

Pattanaik (2009), studied on the implementation of NREGS in Hoshiarpur district. The primary data was collected from 10 village panchayats of the two blocks i.e. Mahilpur and Dasus of Hashiarpur during the financial year 2007 – 2008.

The researcher states that initial findings of the study shows that the scheme has been successful in achieving the equity, while its efficiency is still a question to be efficiently dealt by the implementers of the programme the better nexus and coordination between the government and the panchayats would enable efficient implementation of the scheme at the village level.

Significance of the NREGS

Singh (2008), states that with the experience and learning of the past two years, NREGA will be more effectively implemented. The act covered 200 districts in its first phase and was extended to 330 additional districts in 2007-2008. The author lists out the significance of NREGA thus. It creates a social safety for the vulnerable. It adds a dimension of equity to the process of growth. It creates right-based frame work for wage employment and the right to demand employment in a time bound manner.

The author has presented the salient features of the act as follows. The scheme has a right based frame work and it has time bound guarantee which provides employment within 15 Days. It provides opportunity for women empowerment. The scheme has got worksite facilities such as crèche, drinking water and shade. Social audits have been done by Gram Sabha. All accounts and records relating to the scheme are to be made available to any person on demand. There is a list of permissible work and has a definite funding procedure.

The author has also stated that the scheme has reached out to the rural poor, 117.54% of BPL rural households have benefited from the scheme. There is increased women workforce participation ratio. SC/ST households 62% have employment under this scheme. All the above features and significance are presented by the author as the design of the scheme by the government.

Awareness on the Scheme

Singh (2008), conducted a study. It was published in YOJANA. The author took up Sonbhadra which is the most backward district in Uttar Pradesh. The author concludes after the study as follows" In view of the cited Scenario and problems, we can unhesitatingly say that there is a huge need for spreading awareness in this area. Only awareness can save them from the unscrupulous village and district officials.

Rao (2008), conducted a study on the NREGA. The study was carried out in Raichur district of Karnataka and Anantpur district of Andhra Pradesh in May – September 2007 to access the process of awareness of NREGA in the sample districts. The role of the civil society was aptly acknowledged in creating awareness. Further the author suggests the following for creating better awareness. Community radio concepts can effectively be used to give information to the target population. Local associations and teachers can be roped support the awareness.

Impact of NREGS

Mamidipatty Rajanna and Gundeti Ramesh (2009), studied the impact of NREGS in 22 districts in Andra Pradesh by selecting 500 beneficiaries. Out of the beneficiaries 68.6% of them were women and the rest were men. The objective of the study was to know the impact of NREGP in the area. At the end of the study the following finding were arrived. NREGP increased the economic conditions by reducing the income imbalance in rural area, reduction of wage differences by creating equal wages to male and female workers, reduced the migration level and helped to reduce seasonal unemployment. The study reveals that the beneficiaries expressed the following changes in the programme in order to be more comprehensive. Effective social audit is necessary to eliminate bogus beneficiaries. At the field level the qualified persons require to maintain the accurate records of the beneficiaries and nature of the worker should be amicable to all the beneficiaries who are willing to participate in this programme.

Women and Childcare

Sudha Narayan (2008), carried out a survey on women and childcare in the NREGA works in viluppuram district. The study was conducted in 11 villages and covered about 104 workers. The objective of the study was to find the changes in the lives of women involved in the NREGA works. The author states that NREGA holds a powerful prospect of bringing major changes in the lives of women. This is especially true in a state like Tamilnadu. Where women constitute an over whelming proportion more than 80 per cent of NREGA workers. At the same time, however, some significant challenges frustrate this transformative promise of NREGA. One of them is the issues of childcare. The findings indicate that childcare is a significant problem for many of the young mothers with children below the age of three years. However the scheme plays a positive role in the lives of women. The researcher concludes that provision of effective childcare facilities like the crèches at NREGA worksites is an important action to be taken.

Tamilnadu – A report (2008), published in YOJANA August states. Employment has been generated on a massive scale. While the programme was at a virtual standstill last year (in 2006-08) employment generation has surged during the last few months. The average job card holders in villupuram have already been employed for nearly 25 days since 1 April 2007. Nearly 70 per cent of all rural households in the district have a job card. More than 80 percent of NREGA workers in villupuram are women. In most villages, workers know very little about their entitlements under NREGA. Very few worksites had child care facilities of any sort, even when children were presented at the site.

Social Audit

Siwach and Sunil (2009), selected two districts in Haryana under NREGA for the study. Out of the 7 blocks, the researcher took Sirsa block consisting of 54 villages for the analysis of the impact of Social Audit. The basic aim of the study was to investigate the impact of Social Audit in the selected villages.

The author concludes that the NREGS, by and large, has the potential not only to strengthen social security in India, but also strengthens community's mobilization to ensure better responsiveness of local government to communities needs and priorities.

3

Research Methodology

India is the second most populated country in the world. It is highly impossible to give employment to all the people in the country. However the government has to catter to the needs of the people. A scheme one such as the NREGS is the most wanted of all to the rural people as it provides employment and wages. The researcher has taken this scheme for his study.

This chapter deals with the methodology adopted for the study by the researcher. It includes the significance and scope of the study its aim and objectives, research assumptions, conceptual and operational definitions, the researcher design, description of the respondents of the study selected by the researcher, variables, tools of data collection, pilot study, pre testing, limitations of the study and the outline of the presentation of the various chapters of the researcher report.

Statement of the Problem

India is the largest democratic country with rich and varied culture and life styles. There are industrious cities and fertile villages. The villagers depend on agriculture for their living. More than 80% of the Indians live in villages. When agriculture fails them, they hurl in poverty. They central and state governments have implemented various schemes to eradicate the poverty of the rural people. National Rural Employment Guarantee Scheme (NREGS) is one such a scheme which has gained popularity in recent times. It is one of the schemes that has reached the people directly and is popularly known as 100 days employment scheme.

The scheme has gained popularity among the poor and has many salient features. Has this scheme reached the people. This is a key point to be researched upon. More over the study on this scheme becomes essential as it has affected the rural people and agricultural works both directly and indirectly and in a positive and negative way. These should be studied closely to identify the negative aspects and the central reason behind them. So that they can be rectified in order to make the scheme more successful.

The implementation of the scheme nationwide has many practical difficulties. Only a direct research with those who help in implementing the scheme and the beneficiaries will help to remove these difficulties.

Significance of the Study

This research becomes significant since it studies the effects of the NREGS on the individual, society and economic status of the rural people, both directly and indirectly. The study also helps in identifying the defects of the scheme and suggests ways to rectify them. Hence this research becomes important. This research also reflects the social status of the people, effects of the scheme on agriculture and the present situation of the rural people therefore it can be called as the mirror of the society.

Scope of the Study

The research tries to analyse the effects of the NREGS in the 20 panchayats that comes under the Thirumanur Union of the Ariyalur District. It presents a vivid picture with the statistical data collected from the target area.

The target area has agricultural land of both wet and dry nature. All communities. (SC, BC, MBC) of people live in this area. They are dependent on agriculture for their living.

The researcher has taken the beneficiaries (Workers), Farmers and those who implement the Scheme (Village Presidents and MNP) as the respondents and subjects of the study.

A careful effort has been taken to prepare a questionnaire that covers the economic and social status of the people, education and condition of the family. The research also studies the salient features of the scheme, its implementation, works and wages, measurements and social audits. The study involves direct interview method with detailed questionnaire that studies the scheme from different dimensions.

The researcher presents suggestions to make the scheme more effective. Since this study suggests ways to implement the scheme without affecting the agriculture, which is the lifeline of the Indian economy. It stands as the tool for the government to develop this scheme as well as many more such Schemes without affecting any of the standards in the society in the near future.

Area Profile Ariyalur District

District Profile

Ariyalur district came into existence by bifurcating Perambalur as per G.O.Ms.No.683 Revenue RA1(1) Department dated 19.11.07. It is bounded on the North by Cuddalore, South by Thanjavur, East by Cuddalore and Thanjavur and West by Perambalur and Tiruchirapalli districts. The new Ariyalur district is functioning from 23.11.2007Ariyalur district consists of 2 division's viz., Ariyalur and Udayarpalayam, three Taluks viz., Ariyalur, Udayarpalayam and Sendurai and six blocks.

Brief History of the District

In 1741 the Marathas invaded Tiruchirappalli and took Chanda Saheb as captive. Chanda Saheb succeeded in securing freedom in 1748 and soon got involved in famous war for the Nawabs place in the Carnatic against Anwardeen, the Nawab of Arcot and his son Mohammed Ali.

Mohammed Ali annexed the two palayams of Ariyalur and Udayarpalayam located with troops were in the Ariyalur district on the grounds of default in payment of Tributes and failure to assist him in quelling the rebellion of Yusuf Khan. In November 1764, Mohammed Ali represented the issue to Madras Council and obtained military assistance on 3rd January 1765. The forces led by Umdat-Ul-Umara and Donald Campbell entered Ariyalur and captured it. The young Poligar together with his followers there upon fled to Udayarpalayam. On the 19th January the army marched upon Udayarpalayam. The Poligar's troops were defeated and the playams were occupied. The two poligars fled their town and took refuge in Tharangampadi, then a Danish Settlement. The annexation of the palayam gave the Navab un-interrupted possession of all his territories extending Arcot to Tiruchirapalli.

The history followed was a power struggle between Hyder Ali and later Thippu Sultan with the British. After the death of Thippu Sultan the English took the civil and military Administration of the Carnatic in 1801. Thus Tiruchirappalli came in to the hands of the English and the District was formed in 1801. In 1995 Tiruchirappalli was trifurcated and the Perambalur and Karur districts were formed. Perambalur district was divided into Perambalur and Ariyalur district in the year 2001 and merged with Perambalur in the year 2002. Then now the district is bifurcated from Perambalur and .now functioning from 23.11.2007.

Physical Features

As per 2001 census, the population of Ariyalur is 695524, with male 346763 and female 348761. Ariyalur District is centrally located in Tamil Nadu and is 265 K.M. away in southern direction from Chennai. The District has an area of 1949 Sq.Km.

It is an inland district without coastal line. The District has Vellar River in the North and Kollidam River in the South and it has no well marked natural divisions.

Industry

Five major Cement factories in the district reveal the abundant deposit of limestone. The availability of Lignite at Jayankondam and nearby places is a gift by Mother Nature. The Fossil is said to have been a national asset according to Geologists.

Agriculture

Sugar cane is grown as a major commercial crop. One private sugar factory near keelapalur is functioning in the district with a capacity of crushing 3000 Tonnes per day. One of the main crops in Ariyalur district is cashew. The pre-dominate soil in the district is red sanding with scattered packers of black soil. The soil in the district is best suited for raising dry crops. The district has a high means of temperature and low degree of humidity.

Aim of the Study

The aim of the research is to study the impact of NREGS on the social and economic conditions of the rural people.

Specific Objectives of the Study

1. To study the socio-economic background of the beneficiaries under the National Rural Employment Guarantee Scheme (NREGS) in Ariyalur District.
2. To study the awareness regarding the NREGS among the respondents.
3. To evaluate the usefulness of NREGS in study area.
4. To study the effect of NREGS on agriculture in the study area.
5. To evaluate if the objectives of the NREGS are achieved.
6. To find out whether NREGS helps to promote the infrastructure of the villages.
7. To find out the difference in the standard of living of the village people before and after implementation of NREGS.
8. To suggest ways and means to improve NREGS.

Background Variables

i) Gender

ii) Age
iii) Marital Status
iv) Educational qualification
v) Religion
vi) Community
vii) Family type

Key Variables

1. Salient features of the Programme
2. Annual Income of the Individual
3. Employment opportunities
4. Type of Farmers
5. Awareness on the Scheme
6. Worker scarcity for agricultural work.
7. Implementation of the Scheme.

Assumptions

1. People under the NREGS scheme have higher wages than the people involved in the agricultural work.
2. The Agricultural works had more labourers before the implementation of NREGS than after the implementation of the scheme.
3. The involvement of women labourers in agricultural works has reduced after the implementation of NREGS than before.
4. People with higher level of education are likely to have a higher level of awareness on the scheme when compared to people with lower level of education.
5. People with higher age have less involvement in the scheme than the people with lower age who have more involvement.
6. People of the rural area get higher employment opportunity through NREGS than before its implementation.
7. People with higher tendencies to migrate in search of work fail to register in the NREGS than the people with lesser tendencies to migrate.

8. The scheme has reduced poverty among the people when compared to agricultural work.

Conceptual Definitions

Village

"Village" means a village specified by the Governor by public notification to be a village for the purposes of this part and includes a group of villages so specified.

Panchayat

"Panchayat" means in institution (by whatever name called) of Self-government constituted under article 243B, for the rural areas;

Gram Sabha

"Gram Sabha" means a body consisting of persons registered in the electoral rolls relating to a village comprised within the area of panchayat at the village level;

NREGS

NREGS is a historic employment scheme in India for providing 100 days guaranteed wage employment for all employment seekers above 18 years of age and willing to do work and convert rates on unskilled manual work. The scheme came into force on 5th September 2005 in 200 districts in India and extended to another 130 districts later.

Beneficiary

A beneficiary is one who is benefited by something. In the study it refers to a person who gets 100 days of employment from the NREGS and wages due to him through the scheme.

Employment Opportunity

Employment opportunity in the study refers to the opportunities in various field of work such as agriculture, NREGS and other works. It also refers to opportunities for all communities of people living in the target area.

Wage

Wage can be defined as the money paid to a worker on daily basis depending on the amount of work put in by the individual.

Farmer

A person who operates a farm. A farmer is a person who raises living organisms for food or raw materials. A person who works the land or who keeps livestock, especially on a farm.

Operational Definitions

Socio-economic Condition

Socio-economic condition of the people is a key point to be noted in the study. The condition of the people in the society and in economic standards before and after the implementation of the scheme is being rested through different questions asked to the respondents.

Awareness about the Programme

Thc Success of any programme lies in the awareness of the people about it. Awareness in the study considers the various methods adopted to create awareness and the reach of the methods to create awareness and the reach of the methods to the last member of the society.

Involvement of People

The study takes into consideration the involvement of the people. By this term the researcher means the measures carry out to find if the people do really like the scheme and are benefited by it.

Scarcity of Agricultural Labourer

Scarcity of agricultural labourer means the demand for people for agricultural work, which causes agriculture to suffer. It does not mean the lack of labourers because there are enough labourers but their involvement in agricultural work has become less due to lower wages.

Pilot Study

The researcher had a deep longing to make a study on one such a popular scheme implemented by the government. The researcher made a visit to the District Collector's office at Ariyalur to gather initial statistical information and necessary permissions to carry out the study. Then he made a visit to the Thirumanur Union Office for getting details regarding the panchayats where the scheme is being implemented and discussed with the officials regarding the feasibility, purpose, aim and objectives of the present study. The researcher made visits to different panchayats and gathered useful ideas which helped in the designing of the interview schedule. The researcher also met quiet a number of people informally and had discussions with them regarding the awareness on the scheme, salient features of the scheme and so on. These discussions gave a lot of insights to the researcher which helped in going about with the study.

Research Design

Descriptive research study is concerned with describing the characteristics of the particular individual. Descriptive Research Design has been used for the present study.

An attempt has been made, initially, to describe the background socio-demographic characteristics of the respondents, and then the key variables namely awareness of the people on the scheme, salient feature of the programme, employment opportunity, and then finally to study the association between variables such as employment opportunity, annual income of the individual and worker scarcity for agricultural works.

Universe and Sampling

The universe of the present study includes all the people living within 6 blocks that fall under Ariyalur district. From the total number of 6 blocks, one block was selected by lottery method. Thirumanur block, which was selected, has 36 panchayats. Among them only those panchayats with families that completed the full 100 days under the NREGS were selected by the researcher for the study. There were 20 such panchayats that came under the study. Which had 107 families that completed 100 days of employment?

Census method was used to select the panchayat presidents and beneficiaries (107 families) as respondents and purposive sampling method was used to select the farmers as respondents. In all the 20 panchayats one small farmer, one marginal farmer and one large farmer was taken for the study. (Total number of 60 farmers: 20 small farmers, 20 marginal farmers and 20 large farmers based on official criteria of land holding).

Observational Design

The main source of data for the present study was primary in the sense that the researcher collected first hand information directly from the respondents using the structured interview schedule. However, the researcher used secondary sources of data such as published official reports and other documents, for getting the statistical information about the people registered for the NREGS, funds allotted for each panchayat and the list of works selected for the NREGS. And also the census reports for getting data related to households and population of the area.

Tools of Data Collection

The researcher used a self – prepared structured Interview-Schedule which included the respondent's personal details such as age, gender, education, occupation, income etc, and awareness of the people on regarding NREGS the scheme, registering for the scheme, getting employment and wage and socio-economic conditions of the respondents were included in the schedule.

The schedule also includes questions on the salient features of the scheme and questions to know the effects of the NREGS on agriculture. The panchayat presidents as respondents had questions on administration and social audit.

Pre-Testing

The pre-testing experience would always extend effective support to the researcher to have clarity in understanding various aspects pertained to the research topic.

The researcher went to 6 panchyats in Thirumanur block in order to find out the feasibility of applying the interview schedules for the beneficiaries, farmers and panchayat presidents. The researcher had interacted with all the respondents and was able to add more questions and deleted certain questions. The researcher was able to reframe certain questions after conducting pretest with few beneficiaries, farmers and panchyat presidents.

Data Collection

The researcher went to the Union office at Thirumanur and with their guidance and support met the 20 panchayat presidents. The panchayat president offered to help the researcher in all possible ways. They gave the list of families that completed 100 days of work. The panchayat presidents also introduced the researcher to the beneficiaries at the worksite. The researcher developed a cordial relationship with the beneficiaries and estimated a good rapport with them before the collection of data. The panchayat presidents and beneficiaries gave all the information needed by the researcher. Then he also met the farmers in their fields and houses who also helped open heartedly in the collection of data. The observation in the worksite and lands of the farmers added reliability to the data collected.

The structured interview schedule was prepared in Tamil so that it could be understood by the respondents. The collection of data was done from 19th June to 31st August, 2009.

Analysis of the Data

The data collected were carefully analysed and processed. All the questions in the structural interview schedule were given due importance and were processed into a simple table with the different variables.

Problems encountered by the Researcher

The researcher found it very difficult to travel to various villages in the Thirumanur block. The researcher himself went to 20 panchayats to collect data. It was time consuming to finish the process of data collection. The researcher had to go to their worksites, farms and houses to collect data from the respondents. The three types of respondents such as the presidents, farmers and beneficiaries also made data collection a time consuming process.

Limitations of the Study

The researcher took only those who completed 100 days of work as the respondents. The reasons for the non-completions of 100 days could be analysed only when the other beneficiaries were also met and their awareness of the scheme could not be analysed.

The study could not consider the effects of NREGS on other works. It takes into consideration the effects on agriculture only, as the target area is agriculture dependent and has negligible percentage of other works.

The researcher has limited his analysis of the data to the simple table and has not done any tests.

Chapterization

Chapter I - Introduction
Chapter II - Review of Literature
Chapter III - Research Methodology
Chapter IV - Results
Chapter V - Discussion

Table – 1

Distribution of Respondents by their Age

S. No.	Age	No. of Respondents	Percentage
1.	20 – 30 years	01	5.0 %
2.	31 – 40 years	04	20.0 %
3.	41 – 50 years	10	50.0 %
4.	51 – 60 years	02	10.0 %
5.	61 – 70 years	03	15.0 %
	Total	20	100.0 %

The table above shows the age of respondents. The maximum of 50 per cent respondents belong to the age group between 41 to 50.

Table – 2

Distribution of Respondents by their Gender

S. No.	Gender	No. of Respondents	Percentage
1.	Male	13	65.0 %
2.	Female	07	35.0 %
	Total	20	100.0 %

The gender wise distribution table shows that 65 per cent of the respondents are male and 35 per cent of them are female respondents.

Table – 3

Distribution of Respondents by their Community

S. No.	Community	No. of Respondents	Percentage
1.	SC	03	15.0 %
2.	BC	12	60.0 %
3.	MBC	05	25.0 %
	Total	20	100.0 %

The distribution of panchayat presidents according to caste shows that 60 per cent of them belong to Backward Community. 25 per cent belong to Most Backward Community and 15 per cent belong to the Schedule Community.

Table – 4

Distribution of Respondents by their Educational Qualification

S. No.	Educational Qualification	No. of Respondents	Percentage
1.	Primary	05	25.0 %
2.	Secondary	08	40.0 %
3.	Higher secondary	01	05.0 %
4.	College	06	30.0 %
	Total	20	100.0 %

The education level of the panchayat presidents are shown in this table 40 per cent of them have completed secondary education and it is very important to note that 30 per cent of the village presidents have completed college studies.

Table – 5

Distribution of Respondents by their Family Type

S. No.	Type of family	No. of Respondents	Percentage
1.	Joint	12	60.0 %
2.	Nuclear	08	40.0 %
	Total	20	100.0 %

The above table shows that 60 per cent of the respondents live in joint families and 40 per cent live in single families.

Table – 6

Methods of Creating Awareness

S. No.	Methods of Creating Awareness	No. of Respondents	Percentage
1.	Announcement	05	25.0 %
2.	Announcement and Bit Notices	09	45.0 %
3.	Announcement, Bit Notices and Banner	01	05.0 %
4.	Announcement, Bit Notice and Advertisement Board	05	25.0 %
	Total	20	100.0 %

The above table lists the methods of awareness carried out in different panchayats. Among the respondents 45 per cent of them stated that announcements and bit notices were used to create awareness about the NREGS scheme 25 per cent of the presidents said that only announcement were used and the same percentage of them agreed that announcement, bit notices and advertisement boards were also used for creating awareness among the public.

This table studies the percentage of responses on the methods of verification used to check the applicants. 60 per cent of the beneficiaries produced ration cards and 30 per cent were verified with both ration cards and electoral roll.

Table – 7

Verifying the Application

S. No.	Method of Verification	No. of Respondents	Percentage
1.	Ration Card	12	60.0 %
2.	Electoral Roll	01	5.0 %
3.	BPL Census	01	5.0 %
4.	Ration card and Electoral Roll	06	30.0 %
	Total	20	100.0 %

Table – 8

Number of Gram Sabha Convened to Finalize the List

S. No.	Number of Gram Sabha	No. of Respondents	Percentage
1.	One	12	60.0 %
2.	Two	08	40.0 %
	Total	20	100.0 %

From the above table we come to know that 60 per cent of the respondents have agreed that only on gramsabha meeting was held to finalize the list of works while 40 per cent of them said that two meetings were held.

Table - 9

List of Work done under NREGS - 2008 - 2009

S.No.	Name of the Panchayat	Type of work			
		Water conservation	Renovation	Rural Roads	Total
1	Alagayamanavalam	1	-	1	2
2	Chinnputtakadu	-	2	1	3
3	Kamarasvalli	1	1	1	3
4	Kandiratheertham	1	2	-	3
5	Keelakolathur	-	2	1	3
6	Malathankulam	-	1	2	3
7	Kovilesanai	2	-	1	3
8	Kovilur	-	1	1	2
9	Koman	1	2	1	4
10	Kuruvadi	-	1	1	2
11	Manjamedu	1	1	1	3
12	Melapulur	1	1	1	3

13	Parpanacheri	-	-	2	2
14	Poondi	-	1	2	3
15	Sullangudi	-	2	1	3
16	Thirumalaipadi	1	1	1	3
17	Varanavasi	1	1	1	3
18	Villupankurichi	1	1	-	2
19	Venganoor	1	1	1	3
20	Vettriyur	-	2	1	3
	Total	12	23	21	56

Source: from District Collector Officer, Ariyalur

The table above shows that among the 20 panchayats, 23 works were renovation of ponds and lakes. There were 21 works on rural roads and 12 water conservation works were carried out.

Table – 10

Average Proportion of SC / ST working under NREGS

S. No.	Percentage of SC/ST Beneficiaries	No. of Respondents	Percentage
1.	Below 25%	01	5.0 %
2.	25% - 50%	09	45.0 %
3.	50% - 75%	10	50.0 %
4.	Above – 75%	-	-
	Total	20	100.0 %

The above table shows the percentage of SC / ST beneficiaries working under this scheme. Among the 20 panchayat taken for the study, 10 panchayats have 50-75 per cent of SC / ST workers 9 panchayats have 25-50 per cent of them.

Table – 11

Social Audit at Panchayat Level

S. No.	Interval of Sociat Audit	No. of Respondents	Percentage
1.	Yearly	-	-
2.	Half yearly	11	55.0 %
3.	Quarterly	09	45.0 %
4.	Monthly	-	-
	Total	20	100.0 %

This table studies the regularity of the social audits. 55 per cent of the panchayats have half yearly audit and 45 per cent of the panchayats have Quarterly audit.

This shows that the scheme is being regularly monitored and the funds are utilized properly.

Table – 12

Allocation of fund at Panchayat Level Under NREGS – 2008 - 2009

S. No.	Name of the Panchayat	Provident Funds 2008-2009	Expenditure Funds 2008-2009	Balance fund 2008-2009
1	Alagayamanavalam	686000	495784	190216
2	Chinnputtakadu	1192000	767453	424547
3	Kamarasvalli	931000	693898	237102
4	Kandiratheertham	908000	346507	561493
5	Keelakolathur	1103000	613419	489581
6	Malathankulam	1050000	905446	144554
7	Kovilesanai	964000	596527	367473
8	Kovilur	680000	393908	286092
9	Koman	1303000	720997	582003
10	Kuruvadi	921000	498006	422994
11	Manjamedu	962000	500599	461401
12	Melapulur	1185000	893171	291829
13	Parpanacheri	625500	409654	215846
14	Poondi	1074000	1065610	8390
15	Sullangudi	1042000	308272	733728
16	Thirumalaipadi	900000	512010	387990
17	Varanavasi	630000	557303	72697
18	Villupankurichi	626000	324801	301199
19	Venganoor	118000	390467	789533
20	Vettriyur	1061000	487820	573180

Source: from District Collector Officer, Ariyalur

Awareness on the NREGS

The survey on awareness about the NREGS list out various questions and the responses by the panchayat presidents. The presidents have given 100 per cent responses to all the questions. They all agree that they know about the scheme and have attended special training on it. They also affirm that the ward members and MNP and others co-operate with them. The presidents have registered people for NREGS in their villages.

The villagers apply both orally and in written. All the applications are processed in 15 days by the president himself.

All the presidents agree that no applications were refused and Gram Sabha meetings were convened to recommend the list of works. All the presidents disagreed only on one point that is a separate meeting was not convened on the scheme and receipts for the applications received were not issued to the applicants.

Issue of Job card and Approved list of works

The survey also lists the topics on which there were 100 per cent responses from the presidents. The presidents agree that job cards were issued to all, free of cost, with their photographs, in 15 days from the date of registration. There was a meeting convened in the Gram Panchayat to finalize the list of approved works and the finalized list was put on display for the public to see and all the works were selected from the permissible list of works under NREGS.

Execution of Works

The survey on progress of work brings out the responses by the presidents. There are 100 per cent responses all the responses were positive.

Payment of Wage

The topic lists eight questions on the wages provided to the beneficiaries. All the answers by the panchayat presidents were positive and they agreed that the wages were issued to the beneficiaries as per procedure.

Monitoring and Evaluation

The responses by the presidents on the registers and audit were all positive and the register was maintained as per the procedure laid down by the NREGS scheme and audits were done regularly.

Grievance Redressal

From the survey we come to know that complaint registers are maintained in all the panchayats. All the presidents agree that the complaints are disposed within time limits. The presidents also agreed that no help lines were setup for redressing grievances. The presidents 100 per cent are of the opinion that the scheme should be implemented during times of less agricultural works. They also agreed that the scheme reduced migration and provided employment opportunity to all the people.

Table – 1

Distribution of Respondents by Age

S. No.	Age	No. of Respondents	Percentage
1.	20 – 30 years	12	11.2 %
2.	31 – 40 years	25	23.4 %
3.	41 – 50 years	36	33.6 %
4.	51 – 60 years	26	24.3 %
5.	61 – 70 years	7	6.5 %
6.	Above 70 years	1	1.0 %
	Total	107	100.0 %

Table – 2

Distribution of Respondents by Gender

S. No.	Gender	No. of Respondents	Percentage
1.	Male	52	48.5 %
2.	Female	55	51.5 %
	Total	107	100 %

Table – 3

Distribution of Respondents by Age Vs Gender

S. No.	Age	Male	Female	No. of Respondents	Percentage
1.	20 – 30 years	3	9	12	11.2 %
2.	31 – 40 years	8	17	25	23.4 %
3.	41 – 50 years	19	17	36	33.6 %
4.	51 – 60 years	15	11	26	24.3 %
5.	61 – 70 years	6	1	7	6.5 %
6.	Above 70 years	1	-	1	1.0 %
	Total	52	55	107	100.0 %

The tables above show the age and gender of the respondents. It is clear from the table that the maximum number of respondents i.e. 33.6 per cent of them belongs to the age group of 41-50 years and the male and female beneficiaries in the age group are comparatively equal.

About 92.5 per cent of the respondents belong to the working age group between 20-60 years. It shows that NREGS has been successful in employing the right age group for the works and Table No.2 shows that it is equally beneficial to the male as well as the female.

Table – 4

Distribution of Respondents by their Religion

S. No.	Religion	No. of Respondents	Percentage
1.	Hindu	97	90.6 %
2.	Christian	10	9.4 %
	Total	107	100.0 %

The above table shows that the majority of the beneficiaries 90.6 per cent belong to the Hindu religion. It also shows that even the people from the minority community benefit from the scheme.

Table – 5

Distribution of Respondents by their Community

S. No.	Religion	No. of Respondents	Percentage
1.	SC	27	25.2 %
2.	BC	72	67.3 %
3.	MBC	8	7.5 %
	Total	107	100.0 %

Distribution table above shows the community wise difference among the respondents. Among the respondents 67.3 per cent of them belong to the Backward Community. The Scheduled

Community 25.2 per cent and the Most Backward Community 7.5 per cent have also benefited from the scheme. Though there is a vast difference between each community, still when compared with the population in the target area, the scheme has provided equal opportunity to every community.

Table – 6

Distribution of Respondents by their Educational Qualification

S. No.	Educational Qualification	No. of Respondents	Percentage
1.	Primary	30	28.0 %
2.	Secondary	38	35.5 %
3.	Higher Secondary	2	2.0 %
4.	Technical	1	1.0 %
5.	Illiterate	36	33.5 %
	Total	107	100.0 %

The table above states that 28 per cent of the beneficiaries have only completed primary education and 35.5 per cent have done secondary education while 33.5 per cent of them are illiterate.

Table – 7

Distribution of Respondents by their Marital Status

S. No.	Marital Status	No. of Respondents	Percentage
1.	Married	100	93.5 %
2.	Unmarried	7	6.5 %
	Total	107	100.0 %

The above distribution table shows explicitly that 93.5 per cent of the beneficiaries are married and the scheme helps them in the daily expenses of the family.

The above table distribution of respondents by the type of family shows that 82.2 per cent of the respondents live in nuclear family. While only 17.8 per cent of them live in joint family. It is clear that people from the nuclear families make good use of the scheme and the next table also shows that most of the beneficiaries 84.1 per cent are from smaller families, with only 1-4 members in the family.

Table – 8

Distribution of Respondents by their Type of Family

S. No.	Type of Family	No. of Respondents	Percentage
1.	Nuclear	88	82.2 %
2.	Joint	19	17.8 %
	Total	107	100.0 %

Table – 9

Distribution of Respondents by their Family Size

S. No.	Family Size	No. of Respondents	Percentage
1.	1 – 4 Members	90	84.1 %
2.	5 – 8 Members	13	12.2 %
3.	More than 8 member	4	3.7 %
	Total	107	100.0 %

Table – 10

Distribution of Respondents by their Occupation

S. No.	Type of Occupation	Before NREGS	Percentage	After NREGS	Percentage
1.	Agricultural Labourers	70	65.4 %	25	23.4 %
2.	Own agricultural	20	18.7 %	8	7.5 %
3.	Others works	17	15.9 %	-	-
4.	NREGS works	-	-	74	69.1 %
	Total	107	100.0 %	107	100.0 %

Occupation wise distribution table shows a very salient point about the scheme. The table clearly shows that people who were agricultural labourers (70) and even those who had their own agricultural land (20) have opted to work under the scheme. About (74) of the respondents have left agricultural work and have joined the NREGS scheme. This study shows that agricultural labour has been affected by the scheme. Even the (17) who have done others works before the scheme have left them and joined the scheme after its implementation.

Table - 11

Employment Opportunity of the Respondents

S. No.	Type of Occupation	Before NREGS	Percentage	After NREGS	Percentage
1.	5 – 10	5	4.7 %	-	-
2.	10 – 15	89	83.2 %	10	9.3 %
3.	15 – 20	13	12.1 %	80	74.8 %
4.	20 – 25	-	-	17	15.9 %
	Total	107	100.0 %	107	100.0 %

The above table studies the employment opportunity of the respondents before and after the implementation of the scheme. Maximum number of respondents have expressed that NREGS has given them more number of days of employment per month. (89) of them have said that they had 10-15 days of employment per month before the scheme and (80) of them have agreed that the days of employment have increased to 15-20 days per month after the implementation of the scheme.

Table - 12

Income Variation Before and After NREGS

S. No.	Annul Income of the Individual	Before NREGS	Percentage	After NREGS	Percentage
1.	10,000 – 12,000	7	6.6 %	-	-
2.	12,000 – 14,000	78	72.9 %	13	12.2 %
3.	14,000 – 16,000	18	16.8 %	71	66.4 %
4.	16,000 – 18,000	4	3.7 %	14	13.0 %
5.	Above – 18,000	-	-	9	8.4 %
	Total	107	100.0 %	107	100.0 %

The above table shows clearly that the annual income of the beneficiaries has increased after the implementation of the scheme. The maximum number of respondents (78) have stated that their annual income was 12,000 – 14,000 before the scheme and (71) among (107) accepted that their annual income has increased to 14,000-16,000 after the implementation of the scheme.

Table - 13

Family Expenditure Per Year

S. No.	Spending per Year	No. of Respondents	Percentage
1.	***Food***		
	Below – 5,000	21	19.6 %
	5,000 – 7,500	82	76.6 %
	7,500 – 10,000	04	3.8 %
	Above – 10,000	-	-
2.	***Clothes***		
	Below – 1,000	20	18.6 %
	1,000 – 2,000	62	58.0 %
	2,000 – 3,000	25	23.4 %
	3,000 – 4,000	-	-
3.	***Education***		
	Below – 1,000	40	37.4 %
	1,000 – 2,000	52	48.6 %
	Above – 2,000	15	14.8 %
4.	***Medicine***		
	Below – 1,000	48	
	1,000 – 2,000		5444.8 %
	2,000 – 3,000	05	50.5 %
	Above – 3,000	-	4.7 %
	Total	107	107 %

The above table studies the expenditure pattern of the respondents. The respondents 76.6 per cent spend at an average 500 – 7500 rupees per year on food. Their spending on clothes ranges from 1000 to 2000 rupees per year. The maximum number of respondents 86 per cent spend below 2000 rupees on education and 95.3 per cent spend the same amount on medicine. The above facts show clearly that their spending on basic needs is very meager.

Table - 14

Wage and Working Hours

S. No.	Type of Work	Working Hours		Wage	
		Male	Female	Male	Female
1.	Agricultural Works	5 Hours	5 Hours	100	50
2.	NREGS works	7 Hours	7 Hours	80	80

The above table explains the working hours and wage of the respondents in agricultural works and in NREGS works. The working hours have increased from 5 to 7 hours in the NREGS works. The wages for the men have reduced by 20 rupees whereas for the women it has increased by 30 rupees. There is equal wage for men and women in the NREGS works. The differences in the wages and working hours have not affected the involvement of people in NREGS works as they have regular work.

From the above table we also come to the conclusion that the male workers get fewer wage in the NREGS works comparing to agricultural works.

Whereas the female workers get more wages through NREGS comparing to agricultural works. The female workers benefit more from this scheme.

Table - 15

Saving and Debts

S. No.	Particular	No. of Respondents	Percentage
1.	***Saving Habit***		
	Saving	80	74.8 %
	Not Saving	27	25.2 %
2.	***Saving Money Through***		
	Post Office	17	15.9 %
	Self Help Group (SHG)	33	30.9 %
	Others	30	28.0 %
3.	***Details of Debt***		
	Debt	73	68.2 %
	No Debt	34	31.8 %
	Total	107	100 %

The savings and Debts table shows that about 74.8 per cent of the respondents have the habit of saving and 58.9 per cent of the respondents prefer saving through, Self help groups and other methods rather than postal saving schemes. More than half 68.2 per cent of the respondents also agree that they also have small debts. It is clear from table No. 13 and 15 that the scheme helps them to meet their daily expenses.

Table – 16

Respondents Having Movable Assets

S. No.	Particulars	No. of Respondents	Percentage
1.	Fan	91	85.0 %
2.	Grinder	51	47.6 %
3.	Mixe	27	25.2 %
4.	Television	81	75.7 %
5.	Radio	36	33.6 %
6.	Bicycle	101	94.3 %
7.	Motor cycle	10	9,3 %
8.	Bullock cart	2	1.8 %
9.	Cattle's	68	63.5 %

The above table shows the movable assets owned by the respondents. The maximum number of respondents has only essential assets like fan, TV. Bicycle and Cattle's. Very few of them own comforts like motor cycle and mixe.

Table – 17

Respondents Having Immovable Property

S. No.	Particulars	No. of Respondents	Percentage
1.	***Land***		
	Own Land	24	22.4 %
	Land less	83	77.6 %
2.	***Type of House***		
	Thatched	47	43.9 %
	Tiled	36	33.7 %
	Concrete	24	22.4 %
3.	***Electrification***		
	Electrified	101	94.4 %
	Non – Electrified	6	5.6 %

4.	***Drinking Water***		
	Hand Pumb	17	15.9 %
	Street Tap	90	84.1 %
5.	***Toilet***		
	Own House Toilet	32	30.0 %
	Open Toilet	75	70.0 %

The study about the immovable property reveals the following facts. The maximum number of beneficiaries 77.6 per cent is landless. The same percentage of them lives in thatched 43.9 per cent and tiled 33.7 per cent houses. They have the free electrification done by the government and many of them use open toilets and street taps for drinking water.

Table – 18
Participation of Physically Challenged

S. No.	Type of People	No. of Respondents	Percentage
1.	Physically challenged	2	1.8 %
2.	Normal	105	98.2 %
	Total	107	100 %

The above table shows that the physically challenged people are also benefited by the NREGS scheme.

Table – 19
Gram Sabha Meeting

S. No.	Particular	No. of Respondents	Percentage
1.	Participants	38	35.5 %
2.	Non-Participants	69	64.5 %
	Total	107	100 %

Table – 20
Method of Registration

S. No.	Particular	No. of Respondents	Percentage
1.	Written	71	66.4 %
2.	Oral	36	33.6 %
	Total	107	100 %

The above tables bring out the fact that only 35.5 per cent of the beneficiaries attend the Gram Sabha meeting while 64.5 per cent do not participate in the meetings The table also shows that 66.4 per cent of the beneficiaries register for the work in writing. The scheme is flexible in accepting even the oral registration.

Table - 21

Awareness on Salient Features of the Scheme

S. No.	Salient Features of the Scheme	Know	Percentage
1.	Free medical Treatment for those injured during the work	105	98.1 %
2.	50 per cent of the wage will to be given during the period of treatment	105	98.1 %
3.	There should be an open administration	100	93.4 %
4.	In case of any accident or death during work 25,000/- to be given as compensation	104	97.1 %
5.	The work should be in accordance with Right Information Act.	75	70.0 %
6.	Aged people and Physically Challenged to be allotted suitable work.	100	93.4 %
7.	Social audit reports to be displayed for the public to see	60	56.0 %

The salient features table shows that the people are aware of the benefits of the scheme. We can come to the conclusion that most of the beneficiaries are aware about the salient features of the programme.

Their awareness about openness of administration right to information act, work to be allotted for physically challenged and aged people and audit reports are very little since it does not personally concern them.

Table - 22

Facilities at Worksite

S. No.	Facilities at worksite	Yes	No	Total
1.	Drinking water	107	-	107
2.	Creche	107	-	107
3.	First Aid	101	6	107
4.	Shade	107	-	107

From the table above we come to a conclusion that facilities like drinking water, crèche and shades are given to all the beneficiaries in the target area. A few respondents (6) have said that first aid was not given properly. Whereas majority of them (101) have accepted that all the facilities were provided.

Table – 23

Fulfillment of 100 days of Employment

S. No.	No of Person in a family jointly fulfilled the 100 days	No. of Respondents	Percentage
1.	Single person	20	18.7 %
2.	Two person	61	57.0 %
3.	Three person	21	19.6 %
4.	Four person	5	4.7 %
	Total	107	100.0 %

The table above shows that the scheme provides an opportunity for the beneficiaries to arrange a substitute from their family when they are unable to attend the work. The family members can compensate and complete the 100 days work. The real beneficiary in the scheme is the family. From the table we come to know that (61) respondents have expressed that two persons of the same family completed the 100 days. This provides opportunity for substituting during times of sickness and other personal reasons. So that the family gets 100 full days of work and wages to manage the family expenses.

Awareness, Registration, Job Card, Employment and wages (100 per cent responses from the beneficiaries)

The respondents agree that they all know well about the scheme and its implementation in their village. They all accept that there were awareness programmes held by the panchayat to introduce the scheme to them. The Gram Sabha meetings are held in their villages. They all know how to apply and register their names for NREGS scheme. They accept that they had no difficulty in applying for the scheme. They were also give employment within 15 days from the date of registration. All the respondents have ID cards with photograph and it was given to them free of cost. The respondents agreed that ID card was compulsory in the worksite and it is being verified in the worksite.

All respondents said that the wages were given in cash once a week and as per the procedure.

Awareness on Salient Features of the Scheme (100 per cent Responses from the beneficiaries)

1. The beneficiaries are aware that they must be given 100 days employment per family and they accept that their families were given 100 days of work.
2. The beneficiaries are aware that the male and female workers have equal wages.
3. They accept the fact that the works are not given in contract basis.
4. They also expressed their awareness that machineries should not be used and it was done so.
5. Beneficiaries are aware that women also have equal rights to participate in the NREGS work in the ratio of 1:3.
6. The respondents agree that drinking water, first aid, child care and resting place are provided for the NREGS workers at the worksite.
7. The beneficiaries also know that construction works should not be given under the NREGS scheme and they agree that no such works were given to them.
8. The workers are aware that the worksite should be within 5 kilometre radius from the place of registration and they agree that it was arranged likewise.
9. They agree that when the worksite could not be found within 5 kilometers 10 per cent of the daily wage is given in addition as travel expenses.

Evaluation of the Scheme (100 per cent Responses from the beneficiaries)

1. All the respondents agree that NREGS is very much useful to them

2. They agree that it removes poverty in their family.
3. They are able to meet out their daily expenses and they get employment in their own villages. It also helps them to spend on education, medicine and clothes.
4. The beneficiaries also agree that the NREGS works should be given during days of less agricultural works.
5. The beneficiaries agree that works are given on piece and time basis and for 7 hours only.
6. The beneficiaries agree that the wage details are read out aloud while making payment and it is done at a designated place and time.

Opinion of the Beneficiaries Under NREGS (100 per cent Responses from the beneficiaries)

Positive

1. Beneficiaries get work in their own village.
2. Both men and women get work under this scheme and they also get equal wage. Women do not get so many wages in other works. Even the aged people get work under this scheme.
3. Women beneficiaries say that they could be self dependent with the help of the wages.
4. The scheme helps in managing the daily family expenses.
5. Both men and women welcome the scheme, the scheme is useful more to the women in villages
6. The scheme provides opportunity for compensating the worker with any other family member.
7. The beneficiaries are of the opinion that the scheme is very much beneficial to them as there are no middle men as in contract works. The funds allotted by the government reaches the public directly.

Negative

1. Wages for the men is less and insufficient
2. The piece basis work should be allotted for individual workers so that all the workers give equal share of work.

3. The scheme should be implemented during times of less agricultural works so that there is work throughout the year.
4. Machineries can be used for the most difficult work at the beginning. So that the work is completed quickly and without any danger to life.

Table – 1

Distribution of Respondents by Age

S. No.	Age	No. of Respondent	Percentage
1.	25 – 35 years	13	21.7 %
2.	36 – 45 years	17	28.3 %
3.	46 – 55 years	15	25.0 %
4.	56 – 65 years	14	23.3 %
5.	66 – 75 years	01	1.7 %
	Total	60	100.0 %

The above table we come to know that the farmers of the target area belong to the age group between 25 - 75

Table – 2

Distribution of Respondents by their Gender

S. No.	Gender	No. of Respondent	Percentage
1.	Male	60	100.00 %
	Total	60	100.00 %

The above table states clearly that the agricultural work are done only by male farmers

Table – 3

Distribution of Respondents by their Religion

S. No.	Gender	No. of Respondent	Percentage
1.	Hindu	57	95.00 %
2.	Christian	03	5.00 %
	Total	60	100.0 %

The distribution of respondents table above shows that the targets area consists mostly 95 per cent of Hindu farmers.

Table – 4

Distribution of Respondents by their Community

S. No.	Community	No. of Respondent	Percentage
1.	SC	06	10.0 %
2.	BC	40	66.7 %
3.	MBC	14	23.3 %
	Total	60	100.0 %

The above table states that among the respondents 66.7 per cent of them belong to the backward class. It is thus clear that most of the farmers in the target area belong to the backward community.

Table – 5

Distribution of Respondents by their Educational Qualification

S. No.	Educational Qualification	No. of Respondent	Percentage
1.	Primary	09	15.0 %
2.	Secondary	34	56.7 %
3.	Higher Secondary	05	8.3 %
4.	College	07	11.7 %
5.	Illiterate	05	8.3 %
	Total	60	100.0 %

The above table shows that the respondents are not illiterate about 91.7 per cent of them have completed their secondary education.

Table – 6

Distribution of Respondents by their Marital Status

S. No.	Marital Status	No. of Respondent	Percentage
1.	Married	59	98.3 %
2.	Unmarried	01	1.7 %
	Total	60	100.0 %

Regarding the marital status majority 98.3 per cent of the respondents are married and only 3.7 per cent of them are unmarried.

Table – 7

Distribution of Respondents by their Family Type

S. No.	Marital Status	No. of Respondent	Percentage
1.	Joint	20	33.3 %
2.	Nuclear	40	66.7 %
	Total	60	100.0 %

Regarding the type of family the table above shows that 66.7 per cent of the farmer's family is nuclear in type and 33.3 per cent of them are joint families.

Table – 8

Economic Characteristics of the Respondents

S. No.	Particulars	No. of Respondent	Percentage
1.	***Type of Farmer***		
	Marginal Farmer	20	33.3 %
	Small Farmer	20	33.3 %
	Large Farmer	20	33.3 %
2.	***Type of Land they Own***		
	Wet land	24	40.0 %
	Dry land	13	21.7 %
	Wet and Dry land (both)	23	38.3 %
3.	***Power Motor of their own***		
	Have	28	46.7 %
	Do not have	32	53.3 %
4.	***Cattle***		
	Have	24	40.0 %
	Do not have	36	60.0 %
5.	***Own Farming Tools and Machinery***		
	Have	06	10.0 %
	Do not Have	54	90.0 %

The above table studies the economic status of the respondents. The target area had 33.3 per cent marginal farmers and the same percentage of small farmers and large farmers. Among the 60 farmers 40 per cent of them have wet lands and 38.3 per cent of them have both wet and dry lands. And 53.3 per cent of them have power motors of their own while others do not have. The maximum number of farmers 60 per cent of them has cattle. Among the farmers taken for study 90 per cent of them do not own farming tools and machinery.

Table - 9

Distribution of Respondents by Type of Irrigation

S. No.	Particulars	No. of Respondent	Percentage
1.	Canal	26	43.3 %
2.	Well	10	16.7 %
3.	Lake	06	10.0 %
4.	Oil Engine	09	15.0 %
5.	Rented Power Motor	02	3.3 %
6.	Rain water	07	11.7 %
	Total	60	100.0 %

This table presents the type of irrigation used by the farmers. The maximum percentage 43.3 per cent of the farmers depends on canal irrigation. Some of them 15 per cent have oil engines and still others 16.7 per cent depend on well irrigation. 11.7 per cent of the farmers also depend on rain for irrigation.

Table - 10

Distribution of Respondents by Type of Labourers they Employ

S. No.	Particulars	No. of Respondent	Percentage
1.	Daily Wage	39	65.0 %
2.	Contract and Daily wage	21	35.0 %
	Total	60	100.0 %

The above table states that 65.0 per cent of the respondents choose labourers for daily wages. They are of the opinion that the NREGS affects them because they do not find labourers for agricultural work whereas 35.0 per cent of the farmers agree that they do not have problem when choosing workers on contract.

The above table shows that 60.0 per cent of the farmers accept that there are no changes in the working hours while 40.0 per cent of them say they the working hours have reduced.

Table – 11

Impact on Agriculture

S. No.	Particulars	No. of Respondent	Percentage
1.	***Duration of Working Hours***		
	Reduced	24	40.0 %
	No change	36	60.0 %
2.	***Involvement of Labourers in Agricultural Works***		
	Reduced	51	85.0 %
	Increased	09	15.0 %
3.	***Impact of Migration on Agriculture***		
	Affected	11	18.3 %
	Unaffected	49	81.7 %
4.	***Use of Machinery in Agriculture***		
	More	41	68.3 %
	Less	19	31.7 %
5.	***Type of Deficiency for labours***		
	Male worker	09	15.0 %
	Female worker	38	63.3 %
	Male and Female worker	13	21.7 %

Regarding the involvement of the labourers nearly 85.0 per cent of them agree that the involvement in agricultural works has reduced due to the implementation of NREGS. Labourers show more interest in the works that give them more wages.

The table shows that migration of labourers has reduced 81.7 per cent of the farmers accept this fact. The farmers 68.3 per cent also agree that agricultural have become machine dependent due to lack of agricultural labourers. The most important opinion of the farmers is that 63.3 per cent of them say that there is deficiency for female workers after the implementation of the scheme. While 21.7 per cent say that there is deficiency of both male and female workers.

Impact of NREGS on Agricultural Works (100 per cent responses from the Farmers)

That all the respondents have their own cultivable land and are now cultivating. They agree that they have knowledge about NREGS and its implementation in their village. All the respondents agree that they had enough labourers for agricultural work before NREGS. They also agree that the labourers expect more wages after the implementation of NREGS. All the farmers are of the opinion that NREGS should be implemented during times of less agricultural work on i.e. during summer when there are no agricultural work.

They also agree that there is deficiency for labourers after the implementation of NREGS

Women get more wages in NREGS when compared to agricultural work. The women opt to join NREGS works only this causes a deficiency of women labourers for some of the agricultural works which could be done only by women labouers.

Cultivation in the Target Area

i) Crops Cultivated

The following crops are cultivated in target area 1. Paddy, 2. Sugarcane, 3. Sunflower, 4. Ground nut, 5. Corn, 6. Gingelly, 7. Red Chilli

ii) Crops Frequently Cultivated

1. Paddy – 98 Acre
2. Sugarcane – 86 Acre

The farmers of the target area frequently cultivate paddy and sugarcane in a total area of 184 acres.

iii) Crops Seasonally Cultivated

The Farmers of the target area cultivate sunflower, ground nut, corn gingelly and red chilli seasonally in a total area of 60 Acres.

iv) Total Cultivable land

1. Wet Land – 184 Acres
2. Dry Land – 60 Acres

The target area has a total cultivable land of 244 acres in which 184 acres are wet land and 60 acres are dry land. The cultivation in the wet land mostly depends on agricultural labourers. The implementation of the scheme has created a deficiency of labourers which affects the cultivation in the 244 acres in the target area alone.

Opinions of the Farmers

The data collected from the farmers reveal some of their opinions about the scheme.

1. The farmers suggested that NREGS can be implemented during summer, When there are practically no or less agricultural works.
2. They suggested that machineries can be used for the most difficult and dangerous works.
3. They are of the opinion that age limits should be made compulsory and works should be given to people below poverty line.
4. The farmers also said that the works could be finished in particular time. So that there are sufficient labourers for other works especially agricultural works.

4

Discussion

In this chapter the researcher has presented the salient findings of the present study emerging from the survey and interactions. The researcher has also analysed and compared the findings of the present study in relation to the previous studies conducted by various researchers in the same topic. Subsequently, the researcher has put forth the suggestions based on the study to the various stake holders namely the government, social workers and future researchers.

Salient findings of the study

This section, the researcher has attempted to present the salient findings of the study gathered from all the three categories of people namely the beneficiaries, panchayat presidents and farmers.

Socio – Demographic Characteristics

- o Majority of the respondents 33.6 per cent were in the age group between 41 and 50 years.
- o A little more than half of the respondents 51.5 per cent are females.

- o A vast majority of the beneficiaries 90.6 per cent were Hindu.
- o More than half of the respondents 67.3 per cent belong to the Backward Community.
- o Majority of the respondents 35.5 per cent had completed secondary education.
- o A Very high majority of 93.5 per cent of the beneficiaries were married.
- o Majority 82.2 per cent of the respondents were living in nuclear families.
- o A High majority of 84.1 per cent the beneficiary's families had 1 – 4 family members.

Aspect Related to NREGS

Economic Characteristics

- o Majority of the beneficiaries 70 were involved in agricultural work before the implementation of NREGS while 74 of them joined NREGS after the implementation.
- o A Vast majority of 89 among 107 respondents had employment opportunities for 10-15 days per month before the implementation and a majority of 80 among 107 respondents had employment opportunities for 15 – 20 days per month after the implementation.
- o Majority of 78 respondents had 12,000-14,000 per year as their annual income before NREGS and majority of 71 respondents had 14,000 – 16,000 per year as their income after the implementation of the scheme.

Awareness of NREGS

- o All the respondents 100 per cent were aware of the NREGS and its implementation in their villages.
- o Majority of the respondents 45 per cent had stated that announcements and bit notices were the methods used to create awareness among the public. Other methods used by and large were advertisement board, news papers, Radio, and Gram Sabha Meetings.

- o A vast majority of 86.5 per cent at average respondents were aware of the salient features of the scheme relating to free medical treatment, open administration, compensation, Right To Information Act and Social Audits.

Registration and Job Cards

- o All the respondents 100 per cent were registered under the scheme and job cards were issued to them. Among those registered 66.4 per cent were writes and 33.6 per cent were oral registrations.
- o All the respondents 100 per cent were given job cards and work within 15 days from the date of registration.
- o All the respondents 100 per cent were given job cards free of cast and photographs were taken and no charges were collected for it.
- o All the respondents 100 per cent had stated that there was no difficulty in registering and getting the job card.

Employment and Wages

- o All the respondents 100 per cent agreed that wages were given in cash once in a week.
- o 100 per cent of the respondents stated that men and women get equal wage under the scheme.
- o All the respondents 107 agree that the wage particulars were announced in public and wages were given in a stipulated place.

Salient Features

- o All the respondents 100 per cent were given 100 days of the work per family.
- o 100 per cent of the respondents agree that works under NREGS were not given in contract basis and no machineries were used.
- o All the respondents 107 agree that work site facilities like drinking water, shades, crèches were given.
- o A vast majority 101 among 107 agreed that first aid was given to them at the worksite.

- All the respondents 100 per cent stated that worksite was chosen within 5 km from their village and when it exceeds the limit they were given 10 per cent of their daily wage for travel expenses.

Findings related to Assumptions

- The findings of the survey show that women in the NREGS have higher wages than in the agricultural work. Whereas men who were getting Rs.100 in agricultural work, are only getting Rs.80 in NREGS.
- The findings shows that 70 among 107 respondents were involved in agricultural work before the NREGS while only 25 among 107 were involved in agricultural work after the implementation of the scheme.
- Assumptions states that the involvement of the women in agricultural work has reduced after the implementation of the scheme. The findings show that 63.3 per cent of the farmers have responded that there was deficiency of women labourers after the NREGS.
- The findings on awareness shows that there is no relationship between the educational level and the awareness on the scheme as 100 per cent of the respondents are aware of the scheme.
- The findings differ from the Assumptions and prove that an average of 23.1 per cent from all age groups participate in the NREGs works.
- The findings prove that there has been a growth in the employment opportunities for rural people but it has also created deficiency of labourers in agricultural works which is clear from the responses by the farmers.
- The response from the panchayat presidents 100 per cent proves that the Assumptions that migration has reduced is true.
- The findings show that the annual income of the people has increased from 12,000 – 14,000 per month to 14,000 – 16,000 per month which indicates that the Assumptions is true.

Findings related to review of Literature

- o According to Sharma (2006), the people were happy about getting the job opportunities in their own villages which the findings prove to be true. The author further states that the participation of women has not been found encouraging. The findings of our survey show that a majority of 51.5 per cent women participate in the NREGS works.
- o Tamilnadu – A Report (2008), published in YOJANA and Sudha Narayan (2008) who carried out a survey in Villupuram district conclude that provision of effective childcare facilities like the creaches at worksites should be provided. The findings in the Ariyalur district shows that 100 per cent of the respondents have agreed that water facilities, shed and crèches were provided at the worksite A few 6 among 107 of them have stated that first aid was not given properly.
- o Mamidipally Rajanna (2009), who studied the impact of NREGS in Andra Pradeh States that social audits and accurate records are to be concentrated while the findings from the panchayat presidents and beneficiaries more than half 55 per cent have expressed that social audits were done regularly every half year and 100 per cent of them have stated that records were maintained properly.
- o Singh (2008), conducted a study in Uttar Pradesh. He came to a conclusion that there is a need for spreading awareness among the people. Rao (2007) who made a study of Karnataka and Andhra Pradesh has also stated the same. The findings in Ariyalur district, Tamilnadu (2009) shows that the awareness on the scheme is better when compared to other states and previous years. 100 per cent of the respondents are aware of the scheme and the benefits they would get from it.
- o The findings by Rao (2008), and the findings of this survey conclude that the scheme has reduced migration of rural area to the urban locations.

SUGGESTIONS

Based on the researcher's frequent visits to the villages where the data was collected and through observation and interactions with the general people and based on the findings that have emerged from this study a few suggestions for better implementation are here by submitted.

Suggestions to the Government

1. Men are paid less (Rs. 80/day) in NREGS when compared to other works where they get more (Rs.100 / day) this could be taken into consideration. The scheme has been designed to give equal salary to men and women. The minimum limit can be raised to Rs.100 / day for both men and women. However providing more wages for men would result in better quantity of work.
2. The survey points out that there are people in the group of workers (20 people) who do not involve whole heartedly in the work but get equal wages as those who do majority of the work. In order that every individual gives equal share of work monitoring based on norms could be strengthened which also leads to completion of work and better quality of work. Self Help Groups could also be used to better monitoring.
3. The workers under the NREGS were agricultural labourers previously and agriculture has faced deficiency of labourers particularly women, which could be avoided by carefully planning the 100 days work during times of less agricultural work.
4. NREGS chooses irrigation, rural roads, water conservation etc., as works under the scheme which involves a certain level of danger to the workers initially. Therefore machineries can be used initially to clear out hard surfaces, thorny bushes and for those works that could cause danger to workers.
5. NREGS provides work for aged people and physically challenged people which is very much welcomed by the public. There could be definite works such as arranging water facilities, shades, looking after crèches etc., can be given to them.
6. The findings show that there are no limitations as to the number of days and number of workers for completion of a

particular work which could be standardized. So that the works can be finished in a particular time limit.

Suggestions to Future Researchers

1. The future researchers could make a study on the feasibility of bring out standardized norms for the NREGS works on topics related to monitoring, work allotment, registering people and age limit.
2. The salient features of the scheme have not fully reached the beneficiaries which could separately be taken for study by the future researchers.
3. The study has excluded those beneficiaries who did not complete 100 days. The future researchers can take up for their study those people so that their problems could be analysed and reasons for non completion could be evaluated.

Suggestion to Social Workers

The social workers who play a vital role in Strengthening the government schemes on various level could help in monitoring and implementation of the scheme so that the aims and objectives of the government are achieved.

The social workers could also take up volunteering work of educating the beneficiaries, implementers and farmers on health and hygiene, saving habits and so on. This could further add value to the scheme.

Conclusion

The present study is a humble attempt to describe the important variables such as implementation of NREGS, Awareness on the scheme, salient features of the programme and employment opportunities created by the scheme while considering their socio-demographic characteristics and analyzing the associations among the different key variables. The study has brought out important findings which indicate significant differences between the NREGS works and its relation to the agricultural works, the benefits as against the drawbacks and some valuable suggestions. This study will form a basis for more methodologically sound and rigorous research studies in the broad area of norms related to NREGS works and awareness and reach of the salient features of the scheme.

II. Attitude of Dropout Children of Elementary SCHOOLS

1

Introduction

Education has a tremendous potential to function as an instrument of social change. In fact, it has been put to such use in several parts of the world.

Education and Social Change

What is the role of education in social change? How can formal and non-formal systems of education be used to bring about social change? In particular, what is the role of teacher is social change? Are they agents of social change or leaders of the process? These are all questions that teachers need to answer for themselves.

Education – Economic Growth and Development

The value of education is economic growth and development had not been recognized for a long time. Robert Bald and Gerald Meler reports that "since the mid eighteenth century, economists devoted a large proportion of their labours to the subject of economic development, but only a small fraction of these studies include non-economic variables and these few works are scattered through the mainstream of economic thought.

In fact Dension in his analysis of economic growth in the United States arrived at the conclusion that through between 1909-29 the economic growth in the United States may be traced to the influence of economic factors still the growth during 1929-1957 was more due to education and related non-economic facts than physical capital. The following table which gives a comparison of the GDP, per capita GDP and literacy figures for some of the developed and developing countries of the world highlights and the value of education in development.

Name of the Country	GDP in Million*	GDP Capital	% of Literacy*
I. Developed Countries			
a. United States	1060318	5121	100%
b. United Kingdom	136392	2454	100%
c. Japan	229809	196	100%
d. France	162697	3175	100%
	(1971 data at current prices)		

Name of the Country	GDP in Million*	GDP Capital	% of Literacy*
II. Developing Countries			
a. India	57320	104	31%
b. Indonesia	13957	118	39%
c. Pakistan	11185	204	19%
d. Burma (Myanmar)	2135	79	58%
e. Srilanka	22333	176	75%
f. Thailand	6988	198	68%
g. Brazil	32169	349	76.7%
h. Chile	6124	640	76.7%
i. Jigeria	5310	99	26.3%
j. Ghana	1887	221	26.3%
	(1969 data current prices)		

* a. GDP and per capital figures and from UN statistical year book, 1973 for all countries, PP. 596-598

* b. Percentage of literacy, Economic Survey of the Asia and the Far East, 1972, Unpulications, pp.65.

The table enclosed is very clear. It does not need any explanation. It shows that developed countries have cent percent literacy rates. The value of literate and informal population for economical growth and development needs no further testimony.

Statement of the Problem

Article 28 states parties recognize the right of the child to educational progressively and on the basis of equal opportunity, they shall in particular: make primary education compulsory and available free to all. Moreover article 45 reports the provision of free compulsory education up to the age of fourteen. From the perusal of the above two articles, it is proved that every child is having right to get education at least elementary Education. But majority of economically backward parents are not aware of this and carp the rights of the children by way of sending them for job. But looking from the angle of drop-outs children it is interesting to note what themselves feel on certain factors like Academic, Economic and Social factors.

Problem of primary and compulsory education

The major problem confronting Indian education is the problem of compulsory primary education because the level of literacy has been very low. This shows that primary education has not expanded to the desired extent. Besides, many political, social, religious, economic and geographical factors are creating obstacles in the path of expanding primary education. This problem has been made even more complex by such contributory factors as the curriculum of primary education, problem of school, wastage and stagnation and many administrative difficulties.

Definition for key terms

The important terms in the statement of the problems are drop-outs Academic factor, Economic factor and Social factor.

Drop-outs

Drop-outs are a universal phenomenon which varies from country to country and from region to region with in the same country. A student may attend a course of study for its prescribed duration but: -

(i) May not appear at the examination and discontinue the studies.

(ii) May appear and fail in any one of the examination and discontinue the education.

(iii) May appear, pass but discontinue further study.

The drop-outs not only betray the ambitions of the parents but also prove to be a great wastage of their money, time, efforts and resources of the government which in turn is a great set-back for the nation.

Academic Factor

The school itself appears related to dropout rates, Schools with rigid retention policies, widespread administrative transfers, emphasis on competency testing, tracking and perceived 'unfair' discipline practices tend to have higher dropout rates. Large class size, high teacher turnover, low teacher expectations for student performance, and perceived lack of support for students with academic and behaviour problems is also related to student decisions to dropout.

Economic factor

Number of children in the family, absence of a percent, lack of reading material in the home, parent's education level and family socio economic system are also related to students decisions to dropout

Social factor

India is a pluralistic society comprising population of different socially disadvantaged sections and minorities. These groups are different with each other as far as their life style, attitude towards education and other economic and social problems are concerned. Girls are forced an account of certain circumstances to leave education after a few years because of the prevalence of social evils of early marriage. Many girls and boys leave their studies at a premature age. This and many other social evils are responsible to a great extent for the prevalent wastage and stagnation, which is taking place in the field of education at different stage.

Stagnation and wastages

It was stated in the Hertog Report that the term stagnation was taken to mean keeping a child in one class for more than one year. R.V.Parulkar has explained that schools are established to provide education to children, and not to fail them. No other words, stagnation means the continuance of a child in a single class for two or three years due to failure. This to involve wastage of man's ability and the nation's energy, resources and manpower.

Besides, failure encourages a sense of inferiority in the child, and when children younger than him become his classmates, his abnormality tends to increase. Every year, the level of stagnation in primary classes in between 30% and 50%.

Causes of Wastage

1. Single Teacher Schools – Schools with single teachers make a special contribution to wastage. According to the report of the Indian Survey, these schools have played a significant role in this matter. It is difficult for a single teacher to handle five classes simultaneously. If he goes on leave, the school closes down. This makes the students reluctant in going to school and soon they drop out altogether.
2. Social and Economic structure: India's economic and social structure is of a kind which encourages parents to send their children for general education. Even today, our rural population holds on to the belief that a child should only be educated to the extent of being able to read and write.
3. The child as labourer: Children living in villages are the property of their parent who can compel their children to labour and earn on the fields. For such parents, the money earned the child is more important than his education.
4. Schools without resources: Many schools are almost completely lacking in the resource necessary for teaching and in the absence of these means, the teacher cannot teach. Consequently, the children engage themselves in playing here and there and in the absence of satisfactory results soon leave the school.
5. Lack of space in schools – Wastage also occurs in schools which have only make shift arrangements for housing the children.

Causes of Stagnation

Inefficient Administration

Having thrust the entire burden of primary education on local bodies, the state Governments sleep the sleep of the just. But local bodies lack both finances and adequate means of raising resources and hence they also lack of enthusiasm for the spread of education. If the local bodies serve notices on the local population for the compulsory registration of children in schools, they cannot hope to obtain popular approval in elections. Besides, the presence of inefficient and neither of officials in the local administration further encourage stagnation. Besides, the presence schools are set up in an unplanned, haphazard manner, and this also adds to stagnation. In some areas, there are so many schools that the average attendance in them is only 100. Besides the inspecting staff is also over-burned as it is expected to make a survey of 100 schools every year.

Lack of Money

The main stumbling block is the lack of finance. Local administration cannot spend adequate sums on education. In order to obtain grants from the State Governments, it has to live at the mercy of the Government. Because of this, there are difficulties in arranging not only the salaries of teachers, but even the materials needed for teaching.

Social and Religions Problem

Social and religions problem also contribute to stagnation. In schools which have a dominance of children belonging to a particular caste, tribe or group – such as tribal, scheduled castes, minority language groups, etc., other groups are neglected and this itself becomes the cause of stagnation.

Physical Facilities

The high percentage of stagnation is also accounted for the fact that, from the educational view point, rural areas, hilly regions and forest regions are neglected.

Educational and economic factors

Low standards of teaching, inadequate and unsuitable curriculum, the poverty of the people, etc., are also factors in stagnation. The two later factors help to a very great extent, in lowering the standard of education.

Stagnation and wastage: The Kothari Commission

The Kothari's Education Commission has identified the following causes of wastage and stagnation.

1. The existence of discrimination between children of different ages in a class.
2. The admission of children to classes throughout the year, while this should occur at fixed time only.
3. The irregularity in attending school.
4. Absence of adequate teaching aids and minerals both with the schools and the students themselves.
5. Excessive number of students in classes.
6. The curriculum not being in conformity with needs.
7. The absence of ability and capacity in the teacher to teach through play thus depriving school life of joy.

Removal of Wastage of Stagnation

1. The various sources of human development should be developed.
2. Efforts should be made to discover how the best form of educational development can become possible.
3. There should be planning to ensure that the right kind and quantity of education is made available to every person.
4. Suitable traits should be generated for the development ability.
5. The power to provide facilities should be generated.
6. Manpower should be utilized suitability.
7. Vocational and professional education should be developed.
8. The Education Commission's concept of life-long education should be followed.

9. A clearly defined national educational policy should be framed.
10. There should be rigorous control over schools.
11. The curriculum should be reformed and made useful for life.
12. Arrangements should be made for the training of teachers.
13. Laws should provide punishment for the training of teachers.
14. Audit education should be extended. Education for girls should be expanded.
15. 50% of the total educational budget should be spent on primary education.
16. Classes 1 to 4 should be regarded as a unit.
17. Local cuss should be imposed for financing education.
18. There should be uniformity in education throughout the country.

The Education Committed has clarified that there should be over looking the fact that wastage and stagnation are not illness like headache and fever, but the symptoms of other diseases concealed in the educational method. Of these the main are lack of proper harmony between education and life, and the defective management of schools which fails to attract the students towards the school. Wastage and stagnation are not, in themselves problems. In fact, it is a process, the sources of which whose selfish interests have blinded them to reality. There is no need to solve the problem of wastage and stagnation. What is actually needed is a change in the nature of its source so that these symptoms of a deep malaise may disappear and every child may be able to make his own contribution to the development of the nation.

Period of the Study

The period of the study was five years from 2001 – 2005.

Need for the study

The universalization of the primary education in India is the one of the recommendations of national Policy on Education. There is no doubt the majority of children are completing school education through formal education system. Around six lakhs child labourers are in Tamil Nadu (State Pattern of the project 2003).

At the same time the remaining 5.75 lakhs children are yet to be educated.

The universalization of primary education could be achieved only if any measure will take to investigate the 5.75 lakhs of children. The Government has started District Primary Education Programme (DPEP – 1984) Sarva Siksha Abiya (SSA, 2003) have recently started only with aim of providing equal education opportunities irrespective of caste, religion and so on. Even cent percent enrolment of drop-outs is not possible even thought there are so many attractive schemes like free books, free cloths, free and mid day meals, continent time schedule focusing on vocational skills and so on. As the investigator being a teacher education is SSA, he was stimulated much on how the special school children get education equally like other children.

The investigator wanted to probe the attitude of the drop-outs children towards themselves and other concepts like Academic, Economic and social factors. Hence the problem is stated as "Influences of Academic, Economic and Social factors for drop-outs.

Conclusion

The dissertation has been organized in six chapters. Chapter-I Introductory part of the thesis deals with conceptual frame work different nature of drop-outs children, statement of problem, differentiation of key terms, significance of the study and need for the study. Chapter-II Review of related studies concentrates on attitude and other related areas of special education of both published and unpublished researchers done in India and Broad are discussed. Chapter- III Profile of the study area. Chapter- IV Methodology provides design of the study, the details of the selection and size of the sample sampling technique, tool used. Data collection, statistics used for the data analysis with respect to variables such as sex, community, drop-outs willing and non willing to go to school and drop-outs engaging in nature of the work. Chapter–VI Summary and findings deals with summary implication of the study, recommendation for the study based on the present study in detail.

2

Review of Literature

INTRODUCTION

A review of related literature pertaining to the problem under investigation is a fundamental importance of the research. The research needs to acquire up to date information about what he has thought from which he is interested to take up a research problem. For any worthwhile he is interested to take up a research problem. For any worthwhile study in any field knowledge, the researcher needs adequate familiarity wish the literacy and its resources; only than there will be achievement of an effective search for specialized knowledge is possible. Though a time consuming process, review for related literature is a very fruitful process for research programme. Every investigator must know what sources are available in the field of enquiry which of them.

According to Best (1977) "A brief summary of previous research and the writings of recognized is a familiar wish what is already known and wish what is still unknown and untested. This step helps to eliminate the duplication of what has been done and provides useful hypothesis and helpful suggestions for significant investigation."

Classification of the study

The investigator located 33 studies as related studies. Out of studies 26 studies were conducted in our country and 7 studies were conducted abroad.

Significance of the Related Literature

Research takes the advantage of the knowledge which was accumulated in the past as a result of constant human Endeavour. It can never be undertaken in isolation of the work that has already been done on the problems which are directly related to a study proposed by researcher. A careful review if the research journals, Books, dissertations, theses, and other sources of information on the problem to be investigated are one of the important steps in the planning of any research study. Review of the related literature, serves the following specific purposes.

(i) A careful review helps the researcher in selecting the variables lying within the scope of his interest, in defining and operational zing variables and in identifying variables which are conceptually and practically important.

(ii) It helps the researcher in avoiding any duplication of work done earlier, specifically when the stability and validity of its results have been clearly established.

(iii) It also gives the researcher an understanding of the research methodology which refers to the way, the study is to be conducted.

(iv) The review of the related literature helps the researcher to know about the tools and instruments which proves to be useful and promising in the previous studies.

(v) The advantage of the related literature is also to provide insight into statistical methods through which the validity of research is to establish.

(vi) The final and important specific reason for reviewing the related literature is to know about the recommendations of previous researchers for further research which they have listed in their studies.

Studies on Cognitive and Non-Cognitive Factors

Bombay Municipal Corporation (1967) conducted a study of the incidence of wastage and stagnation and the effectiveness of our educational efforts. The objectives of the study were to determine the extent of wastage and stagnation in primary schools, the reasons for it and their relation to the age of the children. About 6400 children were selected as the sample of the study from seventeen schools from year 1950 to 1958. Major findings of the study revealed that (1) the percentage of children who left school fell from 43.3 to 21.4 in the year 1956 to 1958 (2) 92.9 per cent children left school after one failure in 1957 as against 49.7 per cent in 1950 and 3.46 per cent left school, after passing as against 6.51 per cent.

Sharma, R.C and Sapra C.L. (1969) carried out an investigation of wastage and stagnation in primary and middle schools in India. The aim if the study was to the problem of wastage and stagnation in depth and to ascertain and analyze and stagnation in depth and to ascertain and analyze the cause of it. A sample of 790 drop-outs and 485 stay in cases was selected from ninety two schools, School information blanks, pupil information sheets, and interview schedules were the tools of the study. Information findings of the study revealed that (1) wastage and stagnation was 65% at primary level and 78% at elementary level (2) About 50% if wastage was noticed in class I, itself (3) The rate of dropout is negatively related to the qualification and the preoccupation in case of teachers (4) Drop – outs were usually from nuclear families who suffered the death of one or both parents.

Das, R.C. (1969) conducted a study of the wastage and stagnation at the elementary level of education in the state of Assam. The main objective of the study was to study wastage and stagnation with special reference to primary the study. The study revealed the following results (1) Inspire of a rapid increase in educational expenditure, efforts and facilities, the rates if wastage and stagnation were 77.12 percent at primary and 38.45 percent at middle level for pupils of general. (3) The rate of stagnation among girls was higher than that of boys.

Barua, A.P. (1971) studied wastage in Sibsagar and Golghat sub-division. The major objective of the study was to compare the wastage and stagnation at the primary stage during a period of five years. A twenty percent systematic random sample was drawn which included 113 schools with 2342 pupils from Golghat sub Division and 151 schools with 2872 pupils from Sibsagar Sub Division. Major findings of the study revealed that (1) The wastage at primary stage for boys and girls in Golghat Sub-Division was 80.38 and 78.39 percent respectively. In sibsagar sub division, the wastage for boys and girls was 70.08 and 69.02 percent respectively (2) The level of educational wastage was affected by three factors, viz, drop-outs, stagnated and transfer cases. (3) Poverty, ignorance if parents, poor health of pupils, repeated failure and bad physical conditions of the school were the main factors responsible for the wastage.

Khandekar, M (1974) conducted a study if drop-outs. The major objectives of the study were to find out the socio – economic and environmental characteristics of drop-outs and to determine their motivation fit further education and vocational training. The sample of the study consisted of drop outs in the age groups of fourteen to twenty one years. The investigation revealed that (i) more girls than boys stopped education due to non-economic reasons, (ii) sixty nine percent of drop-outs stopped in their parents. (iii) Financial resources were the main causal factors and (iv) fifty two percent of drop out wished to start education again. (v) Quit a few drop outs had high job aspiration.

Gupta, S.L. (1974) conducted a study of the impact of the un-graded school system on reducing school drop outs and stagnation in primary schools. The main objective was to see the impact of un-graded school system on reducing school drop-outs and stagnation in primary schools survey method was used for the collection of data. Progress on tests and interviews were the tools. Findings of the study concluded (1) The drop out rates for the experimental group, for the project period was 31.7 percent as against the average of 57 percent. (2) The average daily attendance and the levels of achievement of the project pupils were higher

(3). The additional cost involved in the upgraded system was only 1.26 per pupil per year and hence negligible.

Punalekar, S.P. (1975) conducted a study of school drop – out among Harijan children, causes and cure. The chief aims of the study were to study the socio- economic background of the drop-outs and to identify the lapses or short coming on the part of the Harijan families, school system and village community. 198 drop-outs and their parents were interviewed as the sample of the study. Findings of the study highlighted the following major points. (1) The monthly income of 78 percent families was Rs.200 or less.(2) 80 percent children attended school regularly and one fourth regularly attended to home work (3) The main reasons for their dropping out were the economic hardship of the family, ill health in the family or of the child. (4) In 70% cases the decision to drop out was taken by the family while in remaining cases it was by the child (5) The drop-outs had low aspiration level.

Masavi, M. (1976) carried out a study of wastage and stagnation in primary education in tribal areas. Major objectives of the study were to find out the nature and extent of wastage and stagnation and to identify the causes responsible for it. Sample of the study consisted of 104 schools from two tribal blocks of eight tribal districts of Gujarat. Questionnaires were administered and interviews were conducted on parents, teachers and educational inspectors for the collection of data. Findings of the study revealed that (1) the rate of wastage in the first four years of schooling was found to 65 percent. (2) The combined rates of wastage and stagnation in all the fifteen blocks were 83.6 percent and 84.9 percent respectively for the two different cohorts. (3) Wastages were greater amount girls than among boys in almost all the blocks.

Medhi, S. (1978) carried out an investigation into the probable causes of stagnation and wastage among the pupils of secondary schools of Kamrup district. The major objectives of the study were to find out the extent of stagnation and wastage and to find out the causes of these problems. The sample of the study included 100 head masters, one inspector of schools 100 stagnated students and drop-outs and 40 guardians. The study revealed (1) the extent of wastage and stagnation was very high especially in economically backward classes (2) Other causal actors were illiteracy of the parents, their poverty, and lack of study, atmosphere at home and the rate and irregular payments of the stipend.

Raj N.K. (1979) conducted a study of the socio economic factors and interrelation ships among the out-of-school children. The purposes of the study were to enumerate the out of school children in the age group 6-11 years and to find out the socio-economic factor that characterized the out of school children. The non – probability sampling procedure was used on the basis of which 54 drop-outs and 659 left outs were included in the study. Results of the study indicated that (i) there was a decreasing trend in percentage from lower to higher age categories for the left-outs whereas, the corresponding trend for the drop-outs was an increasing one, (ii) drop-outs were found more in larger families, (iii) the percentage of out of school children was higher in those families which were low in family literacy index, (iv) the percentage was higher in nuclear families than in joint families.

Pandey, B.B. (1979) investigated into adjustment problems of adolescents. The sample of the study was 500 students studying in class XI. The tests used were the Adjustment inventory and the test on the level of Aspiration. The findings of the investigation were (i) rural students secured better points in emotional, health and adjustment areas, (ii) significant relationship existed between adjustment and achievement, (iii) urban students were facing difficulty in adjustment in school, heath & educational areas.

Das, R.C. (1979) conducted a study on effectiveness of Teacher Training in reducing educational wastage. The aim of the study was to find out the impact of teacher training on educational wastage and stagnation in primary schools. 743 schools from representative rural districts was the sample of the survey. Important findings of the study were (i) training of teachers had no significant impact on the system of education at the primary school (ii) the training if teachers at the primary level had no significant contribution towards reduction of wastage and stagnation in schools with multiple class teaching (iii) the rate if stagnation in multiple teacher schools with a majority of trained teachers was 60.71 percent against 56.50 percent for schools with a majority of untrained teachers.

Aiskara, J. (1979) conducted a study of educating 'out of school' children. The purposes of the study were to have a preliminary idea about the magnitude of the 'out of school children' and five percent random sample on the 'in-school' children were drawn for the purpose of interviewing parents / guardians. The major findings were (1) the out of school children had a relatively poorer educational, occupational and economic background, (2) poverty and poor educational background stood out as the main reasons for drop-outs and failure to enter school. (3) by and large, parents of out of school, children were eager and willing to send their children to an educational programme that would be suitable and convenient to them.

Seetharamu, A.S. (1980) conducted a study of the utilization for educational facilities by slum-dwellers of Bangalore city in relation to their social and economic backgrounds. The main purpose of the study was to find out the participatory behaviour in schooling in slum areas and the utilization facilities. A sample of 1000 children, 500 drop-outs and 500 stay – ins was selected by stratified random sampling. Important findings of the study were (1) the total dropout rates at the end of Standard I, II, III and IV were 46.20, 24.20, 19.00 and 9.60 percent respectively, (2) mother in unskilled occupation contributed the highest percentage of drop-outs (3) as many as 38.60 percent of drop-outs did not work at home while remaining 61.40 did sine work or the other.

Sarkar, B.N (1980) carried out a pilot investigation on school dropout reasons. The main aim of the study was to ascertain the reasons for drop out and prepare a list of reasons applicable to the rural population of the country. A questionnaire consisting of ninety three questions was administered on a sample of forty six male and thirty five female drop-outs in the age group 6-14 years. Guardians of the drop-out were also interviewed. The investigation revealed that (1) school environment did not contribute to the dropout of students of either six. Domestic work accounted for at least 70 percent of female drop-outs (2) inadequate income for living accounted for two third of the female drop-outs and about 80% of the male drop outs (3) guardian's lack of interest was the most dominant reason applicable to both the male and female drop-outs.

Qureshi, A.N (1980) conducted study of creativity in relation to intelligence, manifest anxiety and level of aspiration are related to creativity (ii) How much and in what way intelligence, anxiety and level of aspiration influenced creativity. (iii) The dynamics of aspiration statistical technique involving analysis of variance and coefficient of correlation were used. The sample was drawn from Firozabad town and there hundred girls of high school and intermediate classes were selected. Creativity test of Mehdi, Group of Aspiration Inventory (Patel). Findings of the study revealed that TEST of Mental Ability (Jalota), STAT by shema and singh and level intelligence was significantly and positively related to intelligence (ii) anxiety appeared to be positively correlated to creativity, (iii) intelligence, anxiety and aspiration level promoted creativity and its components, (iv) aspiration level was related to creativity and its components.

Pillai, G.V., Benjamin, J. and Nair K.R., (1980) carried out a study of drop-outs in primary Education in Kerala. The major objectives of the study were to identify the socio – Economic causes leading to drop outs. Sample consisted of twenty eight lower schools selected from twenty eight educational sub-districts with due representation to highland, middle and costal regions in the state. Four hundred seventy nine house lands were surveyed for the purpose. The major findings of the study were (1) the percentage of drop-outs was higher among boys than among girls (2) Students belonging to SC, ST and other backward communities constituted the majority of the drop-outs (69%) (3) the main reasons of drop-outs were ill health, household work, and poverty in that order, (4) a majority of drop-outs were children of casual labourers.

Vathsala, S. (1981) conducted study of initial drop-outs at Middle school level. The purposes of the study were (i) to identify the causes for dropout and to examine the inter relationship among the various factors related to drop-outs. Thirty drop-outs and thirty staying were selected as the sample of the study. Tools used for the study were the socio – Economic Scale (Pareek and Trivedi) school Adjustment Inventory (Saroji), Self Acceptance Scale (Kakkar), Junior Eysenck personality inventory and Achievement Motivation Inventory (Mehta). The Investigator also used semi structured interview schedule, and schematic differential scale. The study revealed that (1) Potential drop-outs hailed from poor, illiterate, wage earner families, (2) poor achievement in reading and number abilities and failure were associated with potential drop-outs (3) drop-outs were neurotics, had low acceptance and achievements motivation, (4) as potential drop-outs, there was no significant difference between boys and girls. (5) potential drop-outs liked the schools.

Joshi, N.D. (1981) studied the problems faced by certain tribal groups in Trivanderum district. The purposes of the study were to find out the causes of the high drop outs among tribal areas and to find out the causes of the high drop-outs among tribal students. Data were collected by interviewing 400 Kanikhar families and by administering a questionnaire to 54 teachers from eight schools. Results of the study indicated that (1) school facilities within one kilometer were available to 18 percent (2) Tribal families felt that the teachers did not show favourable attitude towards the education of tribal children. (3) Poverty, lack of learning materials, language difficulty, lack of school facilities, in accessibility of schools, ignorance of parents, child labour and parents compulsion were among the factors responsible for their dropping out of schools and for their non-entrance.

A.N. Sinha (1981) carried out a survey of non-enrolled, non-attending and dropout children of 6-14 age groups in Hazaribag District. Fifty schools belonging to fifty villages were sampled for the study. Data were collected through household schedules, school information bank and interview schedules. Major findings of the study were (1) 60.31 percent children were enrolled, 31.68 percent children were non-enrolled and 8.091 percent children were drop-outs in the age group 6-14 (2) The percentage of enrolment increased with increase in family income, however, the incidence of drop-outs was not related to income. (3) The drop-outs were significantly correlated with the number of teachers in the school.

Husain., M. (1982) Conducted an investigation of wastage & stagnation in primary schools of Bhilwara District. The aim of the study was to find out the wastage and stagnation as well as the teaching pupil ration in urban and rural areas. Primary schools of all Panchayat Samitis of Builwara District were selected as the sample of the study. The narrative survey method was used for the study. Major findings were as follows (i) The rate of wastage was higher in the first two classes. (2) Out of 682 primary schools, 506 were single teacher's schools and in these the rate of wastage was also higher (3) The teacher pupil ratio in Rajasthan as a whole was 1: 49 whereas, in rural areas if Bhilwara District it was found to be 1: 26.

Mathur, J.S., Jain S.P. and Rahim, C.A. (1982) carried out an investigation on rural youths from poverty groups: Drop outs and non-students. The investigation was based on the following objectives.

(i) To examine the SES of school / college drop-outs and non student youths.

(ii) To identify causal factors for their withdrawal.

Sample of the study was 1900 respondents selected through multi staged randomized process. Important findings were (i) most of the parents felt that school timings were unsuitable and did not provide adequate opportunity to the children to be helpful in their family education. (ii) The reasons mentioned by non-students for not attending school were poor financial position, parental ignorance, need to supplement family income, frequent migration of parents, unforeseen eventualities such as sickness etc. (iii) in case of drop-outs, parental ignorance, involvement in work, lack of interest in studies and failure in examination were the reasons.

Khanna, K. (1983) conducted an investigation on preparation of reading material for girl drop-outs in Delhi slums. Objectives of the study were (i) to develop need based and interesting reading material for girl drop-outs (ii) to test the effectiveness of the reading material developed for the study Interview schedule. Ability test, Achievement test and questionnaire were the tools conducted on a sample of 103 girls. Major findings were found to be (i) respondents by and large, belonged to nuclear families of seven members on an average and Rs..3000/- as an annual income (ii) the most common reason was found to be parent's education was almost negligible. (iii) the value of R between the three components of reading ability and cumulative learning was 0.71 which was substantial and significant (iv) After exposure to the module, the average score of the girl drop-outs on the questionnaire increased from 7.5 to 13.5 indicating a positive shift.

Devi, K.G. (1983) finds out the problems of drop-outs in primary schools of Manipur with special reference to Imphal town. The investigation aimed at to ascertain accurately the extent and nature of dropout problem and to study various situations. The careers of 54497 and 2927 fresh entrants in class 'A' in 1961 had been followed upto class VII in 1969 in Manipur and Imphal town respectively as the study. The major findings of the study revealed that (i) the difference in rate between boys and girls was 14.26 percent (ii) the difference between the mean rate of dropout boys and girls was 6.30 (iii) the highest rate of dropout appeared in class A (48.48 percent) and lowest in class VI (4.79%) (iv) Poverty, frequent transfer, repeated failures and negligence of parents were the main causes of drop-outs.

Dass, J.R., and Garg, V.P. (1985) studied in impact of preprimary education on drop-outs, stagnation and academic performance. The study was carried out in 18 schools of Delhi Municipal Corporation. For the study of drop-outs, the total numbers of students covered were 10.082 from schools with nursery sections. A sample of 789 class V students was taken to see the effect of pre-school education on educational achievement. Results of the study indicated that (i) early childhood education had a salutary effect in case of the group which was pre-school education (iii) slightly higher achievement was also observed in class V among students who attended pre-primary education.

Rather A.R. (1985) carried out a study on incidence of drop-outs and maladjustments among students in relation to creativity and social structure of the school. Main objectives of the study were (i) to study the relationship between incidence of drop-outs and socio-metric status of pupils (ii) to study the relationship between incidence of dropout and creativity. (iii) to study the relationship between Adjustment of pupils and their creativity (iv) to study the relationship between SES, incidence of drop-outs and Adjustments. Sample of the study comprised 887 students ranging age from 11-14 years. Satisfied techniques applied were t-test, Chi-square test and product moment correlation. Main findings of the study were (i) the incidence of drop-outs was positively related with socio-metric status of the child in the class room (ii) the dropout incidence was significantly related to SES of children. (iv) the relationship between Adjustment and SMS was found to be significant and positive. The same was the case between Adjustment and Creativity (v) Creativity and Adjustment were not significantly related.

S. Subramanyam (1986), studied the problem of school drop-outs with special reference to scheduled castes and scheduled tribes. The main purpose of the study was to identify the relative influence of personal, economic and socio-cultural problem of school drop-outs. A sample of 300 drop-outs in 30 areas covering three districts of Andhra Pradesh was selected by stratified random sampling procedure. Problem checklist was developed to enumerate the problems of drop-outs. The findings of the study revealed that. (i) the problem in the area of personal factors such as Adjustment to the present educational set up are considerably high and this situation is very severe in the case of girls and with regard to children belonging to scheduled tribes. (ii) the economic problem of school drop outs are also considerable high in the case of SC's and ST's (iii) the social problems are also considerably high in case of scheduled tribes (iv) there was no significant difference in the sub areas of economic and social problems and boys are more sufferer in the area of personal problems.

SIE, U.P., (1986) conducted a study of drop-outs and failures in primary classes. The main purpose of the study was to study the causes of drop-outs and failures among 6-14 age group students. The study was delimited to the four regions of the state, namely the middle zone eastern zone, southern zone and western zone. The findings revealed that (i) in all the four developed blocks, the development trend showed that from 6-8 class, 15 percents were drop-outs and four percents were failures (ii) maximum drop-outs were seen among children coming from backward classes (iii) the main causes for drop-outs were illiteracy of the parents, poverty, lack of interest distance of school from home, unattractive environment of the school, indifference of teachers, irrelevant curriculum, lack of physical facilities like water and sanitation etc., in schools.

Dianes, Kaplin, B.Mitchell Peck, Howard B. Kaplan (1990) conducted a study – Decomposing the academic failure, dropout relationship: A longitudinal analysis. Data from a four – wave panel (N = 195) tested in the 7th, 8th and 9th grades and as young adults, were used to estimate a causal model. The model was used to decompose a previously, observed term of 5 theoretically informed mediating variables. The academic failure drop-outs relationship was partially decomposed by mediating effect of low motivation, association with deviant peers and perception of rejection by the students at school. Although perception of rejection by teachers and resistance towards school were, as hypothesized, influenced by earlier negative academic experience. They had no independent effect on dropping out not of their relationship to associate with deviant peers or low motivation. Implications for current practices and future research are also discussed.

Stevenson, R.B & Ellsworth, J. (1991) conducted a study on dropping out in a working class high schools, adolescent voices on the decision to leave. Finding reveals how the schools response, or lack thereof, to student's problem compound their difficulties and create tensions over the source of blame for their failure. However these adolescents also attributed much of their failure of themselves. In revealing the issue of blame, these suburban white drop-outs in contrast to immercify minority youth believed that they must be at fault for failing to conform to the expectation and demands of schools.

Mc.Caul, Edward, et al (1992) Studied the consequences of dropping out of school, findings from high school and beyond. The purpose of the present study was to examine the personal, social and economic consequences of dropping out of school. Drop out differed from graduates with no post secondary education on many personal and social adjustments measures. Results indicated that male and female drop-outs have different personal, social and economic experience.

Flisher, A.J. & Chalton, D.O. (1995) conducted a study in high school drop-outs in a working class South African Community; selected characteristics and risk – taking behaviour. Structured questionnaire data from household heads and adolescent drop-outs in a working class south African Community were used to explore drop-outs characteristics and the prevalence of their risk taking behaviour compared with those attending school of the 548 teenagers sampled 15.9% were drop-outs of these 62.1% left school after less than years. Those still attending to school were more likely to engage in suicidal behaviour, but less likely to abuse substances and (for girls) to have had sexual intercourse.

Jordon, will J., Lara and Mc Partland, James (1996), explored the causes of early dropout among race–ethnic and gender groups.This study used nationally representative high school student data to show race - ethnicity and gender difference in reasons for early school drop-outs and plans for drop-outs to resume their education. Factor analysis shows that separate reasons for dropping out include school related, family related and job related causes as well as influences from peers and residential mobility. White drop-outs cited alienation from school, more often than their African–Americans or Hispanic of both sexes.

African Americans males reported being responded or expelled from school more than the other groups. Hispanic and African American females cited family reasons more often than did white females.

Teachman Joy D., Paasch and **Carver Karen (1996)** conducted the study of social capital and dropping out of school early. A large sample of data was taken from the national educational longitudinal survey to examine the effects of various measures of social capital on the likelihood of dropping out of school early, before 10th grade controlling for indicators of the financial and human capitals of parents. Result indicated that more specific indicators of social capital (patterns of parental interaction, number of times the child changed school) can account for all the effect of attending a catholic school, but only a fraction of the effect of family structure on leaving school early.

3

Profile of The Study Area

DISTRICT PROFILE

Karur District is a centrally located inland district of Tamil Nadu, spread over 3690.07 sq.kms, which was trifurcated from the erstwhile composite Tiruchirappalli District and was formed on 1 November 1995. The District is bounded by Salem District in the North, Tiruchirappalli District in the South, Karur in the East and Namakkal and Erode Districts in the West.

The total Geographical area of the District is 369007 ha. and net sown area and gross sown area are 216422 ha. And 237136 ha. respectively. The net area under irrigation is 71624 ha. The total population of the District as per 2001 census is 11, 81,029 of which 5,88,441 are males and 5,92,588 are females. The sex ratio is 1007 with the birth rate at 21.6 and the death rate at 7.7. The density of population of the District per Sq.K.M. is 281 persons as against the stage average of 429 persons.

The district for administrative purpose has been divided into 5 Taluks (Karur, Kulithalai, Aravakkurichi, Kadavur and Krishnarayapuram) which is further sub-divided into 8blocks viz.,

(Karur,K.Paramathi, Aravakkurichi, Thanthotrimalai, Krishnarayapuram, Kulithalai, Kadavur, Thokaimalai) comprising of 345 villages, 322 village Panchayat and Nine Panchayats.

The District lies in the Southern plateau & hill zone of Agro-climate regional planning with characteristics of semi arid climate. The soil is predominantly red loamy and black soil. The normal rainfall of the District 908 mm, which is less than 946.9 mm, the normal rainfall of the State. The precipitation during northeast monsoon, southwest monsoon and remaining winter & hot weather period account for 52 percent, 34 percent and 14 percent of annual rainfall respectively.

Cauvery is the major river flowing in the region and the composite District has a canal system. Covering just 47 kms stretch and ayacut of 11610 ha. The Ground water resource through tube wells and wells contribute nearly 68% of irrigated area command. The major crops grown in the district are paddy, groundnut, sugarcane and millets. Cashew is the major plantation crop.

There are a total of 47 PHCs in the District of which 37 are additional PHCs, 7 are block and 3 are 24 hour PHCs. The number of primary schools, middle schools, high schools and higher secondary schools are 722, 118, 82 and 67 respectively.

ADMINISTRATIVE UNITS

REVENUE DIVISION

1. Karur
2. Kulithalai

TALUK

Sl. No.	Taluk Name
1.	Karur
2.	Kulithalai
3.	Aravakkurichi
4.	Kadavur
5.	Krishnarayapuram

BLOCK

Sl. No.	Block Name
1.	Karur
2.	K.Paramathi
3.	Aravakkurichi
4.	Thanthotrimalai
5.	Krishnarayapuram
6.	Kulithalai
7.	Kadavur
8.	Thokaimalai

REVENUE VILLAGE

Sl. No.	Revenue Village
1.	Panchapatti
2.	Vankal
3.	Uppidamangalam
4.	Velliyanai
5.	Tharagampatti
6.	Kaniyalampatti
7.	Noiyel
8.	Karur (North)
9.	Malaikovilure
10.	Pugakure
11.	Esanatham
12.	Thennilai
13.	Kadavur
14.	Thammanaickan patti
15.	RasandarThirumalai
16.	Ranganathanpettai
17.	Manmangalam
18.	Coyampalli
19.	N.Pudure
20.	Koundampalayam
21.	Pallapalayam
22.	Kovilure

23.	Nachalure
24.	Iyarmalai
25.	Velliyanai
26.	Neithalure
27.	Mayanure

Panchayat Villagers

Sl.No.	**Panchayat Village**
1.	Karvazhi
2.	Thalaipatti
3.	Venkampatti
4.	Enunkure
5.	Kelaveliyure
6.	Attur
7.	Thumbivadi
8.	Yudaiyappatti
9.	Senkulam
10.	Kattalai
11.	Mettuthirukapuliyure
12.	Thottakurichi
13.	Soundarapuram
14.	Vankal
15.	Jagathabi
16.	Punavasappatti
17.	Porani
18.	Pasupathipalayam
19.	Puliyure
20.	Pallappatti

Particulars	**Karur District**		
	Male	**Female**	**Total**
Total Population	588441	592588	1181029

Agriculture Department

The agriculture department in the district is headed by joint director of agriculture. As the district is mainly agrarian, the improvement of productivity, production and profitability becomes most important objective of the department in the district. Secondly the agro climatic zone of the district is favorable for cultivation of the some of the medicinal and aromatic plants. The district has the largest area under cotton cultivation.

Panchayats

Sl. No	Details of Wards	Total
1.	Hamlets	924
2.	Panchayats	322
3.	Panchayat Wards	1107
4.	Panchayat Unions	10
5.	Panchayat Union Wards	189
6.	District Panchayat Wards	8/12

Street Lights

Sl. No	Details of lights	Total
1.	Tube Lights	27030
2.	Sodium Vapours	2891
3.	Others	453
	Total	30374

Education – District Primary Education Programme

Introduction

District Primary Education Programme has been launched in this District since November 1997. The main criteria for selecting this District are the lower level of the female literacy rate than the national literacy at the time of introduction of District Primary Education Programme.

Aims and Objectives of DPEP

1. Enrolment of all the school age children in the age group of 6 to 11.
2. Retention of all the enrolled children in schools without any dropout.

3. Completing five year of Primary Education with quality.
4. Promoting of Girls Education.
5. Provision of Integrated Education for the Disabled children.
6. Involving the community for the better functioning of schools.

SCHEMES DPEP

Buildings were taken up for construction both by the Public Works Department and the community participation work. 69 schools were benefited under the scheme.

ALTERNATIVE SCHOOLS

In order to provide inclusive education for the dropout and non enrolled children including migrated and child labour children. Alternative schools have been started in all blocks

1.	Karur	6 Centres
2.	Kulithalai	3 Centres
	Beneficiaries	180 Children

SC / ST SPECIAL COACHING CLASSES

To promote girls education, particularly children belongs to SC / ST community, Special Coaching classes were started for the above girl children in 3, 4 & 5 standards. Being the first generation learners, the SC / ST children could not complete the children of the other social groups. But now from February 2002 onwards, SC/ST boy's children have also been included under the above scheme. Disabled children have also been included along with SC/ST children.

Beneficiaries

Total No.of Schools	172
Total No.Centres	342
Beneficiaries SC / ST	9555 (4919 + 4636)
Beneficiaries IED	484 (299 + 185)
Total Beneficiaries	9939 (5218+4821)

TRAINING PROGRAMMES

Quality improvement is one of the major objectives of DPEP. Many of the schools have multi-grade teaching situation i.e., single teacher has to handle more than one classes. The teachers are given following types of training to improve their teacher skills in such situations.

- o To teach more than one subjects.
- o Refresher cum Booster course.
- o English training to teacher handling 3, 4 and 5 standards.
- o Training an Activity Based joyful teaching methodology.
- o Training to newly appointed teachers.
- o Training to teachers who handled SC/ST special coaching classes.
- o Preparation of Teaching Learning Material.

Teaching learning material and infrastructure grant

All the teacher working in Primary classes are provided with the above grant at Rs.500/- every year for purchasing teaching material Rs.2000/- per years sanctioned to all schools to improve the infrastructure facilities.

Early Childhood Education

The ECE centers facilitate the girl child to attend schools by relieving them from the sibling care responsibilities. Being the feeder institution of Primary Schools, the Child Welfare Organizers are given two days training programme every year. Apart from that, the DPEP has also programmed to supply teacher and learning materials at Rs.1000/- per centre.

Integrated Education for the Disabled Children

Universaliation of Primary Education cannot be prescribed unless we mainstream all the disabled children. 9 Special teachers as various impairments are working to cater to the needs of the 384 disabled children. One medical camp was conducted at Karur Block. Similar camps are programmed in the remaining blocks.

Aids and appliances have also been supplied with the help of Rehabilitation Department.

Kulithalai Block

In Kulithalai block according to the census report it has an population of 31,268 in total of which 41% are male and 59% are female. 11% of the total population is below 60 years of age. The total literacy of the block is 69%. Out of the 11,612/- of the job holders 8,042 are male and 3,210 are female. The block has 35 villages and 21 schools, out of which 14 are primary, 3 are high school and the remaining 4 are higher secondary schools.

4

Research Methodology

Introduction

The present chapter deals with the methodology of the study. First section deals with design of the study. The second section deals with the objectives of the study. The hypotheses are presented in section three. The fourth section describes the selection sample. The fifth section explains the tool used. The sixth section deals with data analysis with statistical technique used. The seventh section covers the limitations of the study.

Design of the study

Research design is facilitating the smooth sailing of the various research operations, thereby making research as efficient as possible yielding maximum information with minimum expenditure of effort, time and money. *Kerlinger (1973),* as pointed out that research investigation conceived so as to obtain to control variance.

As shown in the above table, the nature of the study is normative survey. The variables in the study were academic,

Economic, and Social Factors, As the standardized tool was not available, the investigator himself developed a tool, named "Academic, Economic and social factors influencing dropout children. The tool used was 5 point scale to measures the attitude of dropout children. The investigator used the stratified random sample technique in the study. The size of the sample was 100 which were selected systematically out of the total sample 400 in Kulithalai Block. The total sample was sub-divided with respect to sex, community, willing and unwilling to go to school and nature of the dropouts. The collected data was analyzed with the use of different statistical techniques.

Table-1

S.No	Type	Source
1.	Nature of the Research	Normative Survey
2.	Variables	I. Academic factors II. Economic factors III. Social factors
3.	Tool Used	Attitude towards academic, economic and social factors
4.	Sampling Technique	Stratified Random Sampling
5.	Size of Sample	100 dropouts of Kulithalai Block

6. Sub Sample

		Primary		Upper Primary	
I.	Sex	Male	23	Male	: 26
		Female	: 24	Female	: 27
II.	Community	SC	: 21	SC	: 26
		MBC	: 18	MBC	: 20
		BC	: 8	BC	: 7
III.	Willing and non willing to go to school	Willing	: 23	Willing	: 29
		Non-willing	: 24	Non-willing	: 24
IV.	Nature of to work of the dropouts	Daily Wages	: 26	Daily Wages	: 28
		Vendors	: 21	Vendors	: 25

7.	Statistical Technique used	Mean, standard Deviation and 't' test

OBJECTIVES OF THE STUDY

The main objectives of the study to study the Attitude of dropout children among primary and upper primary level in Kulithalai Block towards different factors such as academic economic and social factors. The specific objectives are as follows:

1. To study the attitude of male and female dropouts children towards different factors.
2. To study the attitude of dropouts children belonging to different communities. SC, MBC, and BC towards different factors.
3. To study the attitude to dropouts children whose willing and non-willing to go to school towards different factors.
4. To study the attitude of dropouts children whose nature of the work towards different factors.

Hypothesis of the study

The following hypotheses were formulated to realize the above objectives.

1. There is no significant difference on the attitude among the dropouts children towards different factors such as Academic, Economic and social factors.
2. There is no significant difference between the means scores male and female of dropouts children towards different factors.
3. There is no significant difference among the mean scores of dropouts children with respect to different communities such as SC, MBC and BC.
4. There is no significant difference among the means scores of dropouts children whose willing and unwilling to go to school.
5. There is no significant difference the mean scores of dropouts children whose nature of the work towards different factors.

SAMPLE SIZE

The primary and upper primary dropouts children in Kulithalai Block were the population of the study. They are 400 dropouts children among primary and upper primary level in Kulithalai

Union. Based on the stratified random sampling techniques, the investigator selected 100 samples. The students of standard 9 and 10 were not included in the study. The dropouts children whose were not included in the study. The dropouts children whose were studying from 1-5th and 6-8th standard were included in the study. The names of the cluster resources centre of Kulithalai Block Resource Centre and Strength of the students are given below.

Table-2 Name and Strength of the sample

S. No.	Name and Place of the CRC	Strength
1.	Karur (North)	10
2.	Malaikovilure	10
3.	Pugakure	10
4.	Esanatham	10
5.	Thennilai	10
6.	Kadavur	10
7.	Thammanaickan patti	10
8.	RasandarThirumalai	10
9.	Ranganathanpettai	10
10.	Manmangalam	10
	Total	100

The total sample was sub-divided with respect to sex, community, willing and unwilling to go to school, nature of work of the dropouts children.

The size of the sample with respect to sex is presented in the following table.

TABLE-3 Sample Based on Sex in Primary and Upper Primary Level

S.No.	Category	Primary Level		Upper Primary Level	
		Size	**%**	**Size**	**%**
1.	Boys	23	48.9	26	49.0
2.	Girls	24	51.1	27	51.0
	Total	47	100.0	53	100.0

Table 3 reveals that 48.9% of the boys in primary level, 49% of the boys in upper primary level dropouts children and the remaining 51.1% of the upper primary level and girls of dropouts children. Further the sample was classified based on their community.

Table-4 Sample Based on Community in Primary and Upper Primary Level

S.No.	Category	Primary Level		Upper Primary Level	
		Size	%	Size	%
1.	Schedule Caste (SC)	21	44.7	26	49.0
2.	Most Backward Class (MBC)	18	38.2	20	37.7
3.	Backward Class (BC)	8	17.1	7	13.3
	Total	47	100.0	53	100.0

Table 4 shows that among the total sample 47, 47.7% are scheduled caste, 38.2% are most backward community and sample 17.1% are backward caste in Primary level.

In the upper primary level the total sample was 53, 49% are scheduled caste, sample 37.7% are most backward community and sample 13.3% are backward caste. Further the sample was classified based on the willing and non willing to go to school in primary and upper primary level.

Table-5

Sample Based on Willing and non willing to go to school in Primary and Upper Primary Level

S.No.	Category	Primary Level		Upper Primary Level	
		Size	%	Size	%
1.	Willing to go to school	23	48.9	29	54.7
2.	Non Willing to go to school	24	51.1	24	45.3
	Total	47	100.0	53	100.0

Table 5 shows that among the total sample 47, 48.9% are willing to go to school, sample 51.1% are non willing to go to school in Primary level. In the upper primary level the total sample was 53, 54.7% are willing to go to school, sample 45.3% are non willing to go to school.

For the further analysis the sample was classified based on their nature of the work of the dropouts children in primary and upper primary level.

Table-6

Sample Based on nature of the work of dropouts children in Primary and Upper Primary Level

S.No.	Category	Primary Level		Upper Primary Level	
		Size	%	Size	% %
1.	Daily wages	26	55.3	28	52.8
2.	Vendors	21	44.7	25	47.2
	Total	47	100.0	53	100.0

Table 6 shows that among the total sample 47, 55.3% of daily wages and sample 44.7% of vendors in Primary level.

Tool used in the study

The investigator himself developed the 5 point attitude scale.

Preparation of Preliminary draft of academic, economic and social factors.

As the investigator was much interested on the education of dropouts children throughout at Kulithalai block in Karur District, he went on coining suitable items to measures the attitudes towards different factors such as Academic, Economic and Social factors.

The investigator selected both positive and negative items. To elicit the reliable response from the subjects strongly agree of positive items gets 5 and agree, undesired, disagree and strongly disagree gets 4, 3, 2 and 1 respectively. Likewise, "The negatively items gets 5 strongly agree gets 1 and agree, undesired, disagree and strongly disagree gets 2, 3, 4 and 5 respectively. Accordingly all the statements were prepared. The investigator took care to prepare 5 points scale which deal with significant ideas. Certain item eliciting the same response and repletion of the words in the options were avoided.

Attention was given to have the items uniformly selected from different variables. After perusal of the items, certain items were deleted and certain items were added wherever necessary. After the investigator himself satisfied on the items prepared, it was given to the experts who are interested in this field, their suitable suggestions were carried out. After carrying out all these were 100 items in all three factors such as Academic, Economic and Social factors.

A blue print was prepared to check the items which are presented the following table given below.

Table-7

Blue Print for Preliminary drafts of Academic, Economic and Social Factors

S.No.	Factors	Item Numbers	Total	Percentage (%)
1.	Academic	1-36	36	36.0
2.	Economic	37-66	30	30.0
3.	Social	67-100	34	34.0
		Total	100	100.0

Item Analysis

The Investigator gave the statement of the questionnaire to the dropouts children from Koyudampatti in Karur union. Based on the procedures of item analysis, all the items in the questionnaire were processed. On the basis of the results, the investigator changed some of the items and some of the items were modified.

Ultimately the total numbers of items were 72 out of 100 for the final study. The item selected for the final study are presented in the table given below.

The table 8, shows that the total item selected for the final study were 72 of which items related to factors of Academic are 36.1% Economic 27.8% Social 36.1%. Thus the tool was constructed by the investigator for the study.

Table-8

Blue Print for the find drafts of Academic, Economic and Social Factors

S.No.	Factors	Item Numbers	Total	Percentage (%)
1.	Academic	1-26	26	36.1
2.	Economic	27-46	20	27.8
3.	Social	47-72	26	36.1
		Total	72	100.

Validity and reliability

The investigator gave the questionnaire to the two teacher educators to verify the suitability of the items. Based on their suggestion medications was made. Thus the validity of tool was established. The investigator randomly selected 15 dropouts children from Puliyure in Kulithalai Union in Karur District. The prepared questionnaire was administered to them. After 15 days, the same questionnaire was administered to the same subjects the investigator valued the both questionnaire and found correlation co-efficient between the sets of the scores. The value of co-efficient of the reliability test was 0.87. Based on the result the tool was considered as highly valuable.

Collection of Data

The tool was administered to 100 samples. The selection of samples for the final study was discussed under the caption 3.5. The Investigator asked the subjects to go through all their free time and put the tick mark in the attitude scale under the appropriate place in the questionnaire. The subjects were also instructed to note the positive and negative statements in the tool. After collecting the filled in a questionnaire the investigator second systematically. Thus the data required for the study were collected.

Statistical Technique

The collected data was systematically organized and suitable statistical techniques were applied to draw the precise solution in the study. Mean and standard deviation were calculated to find out t' value is in order to find out the significant difference between the two variables. Percentage was also used to analysis to data in the study.

Limitation of the study

The limitations of the study are listed below.

1. The investigator found very limited research work in the area of dropouts children in journals and survey of research.
2. The investigator confined his study with 100 samples, as it was difficult to identify them.

The forth coming chapter deals with data analysis.

5

Analysis of Data

OVERVIEW

Present chapter gives the details, about the analysis of the collected data. All the data were analyzed with the level of significance of 0.05 level. Percentage, t-test, Chi-square test were the statistical techniques employed in the analysis of the data to draw meaningful generalization. The data has been organized in four sections as follows:-

CLASSIFICATION OF ANALYSIS

The data analysis has been organized in four sections as follows:

SECTION A

This section deals with the analysis on the mean values of the different factors at primary and upper primary level.

SECTION B

This section contains the analysis an factor wise analysis at primary and upper primary level.

SECTION C

This section reveals the analysis on the Academic factors with respect to demographic variables at primary and upper primary level.

SECTION D

This section deals with the analysis on Economic factors with respect to demographic variables at primary and upper primary level.

SECTION E

This section contains the analysis of Social factors with respect to demographic variables at primary and upper primary level.

SECTION A

Mean values of different factor at primary an upper primary level

From the collected data, mean values of different factors such as Academic, Economic and Social variables with respect to sex, community, willingness to go to school and present job responsible for dropouts at Primary and upper primary levels was calculated. The results were presented in Table 5.1 and table 5.2.

Table-9

Mean value of different factors responsible for dropouts in Primary Level

S. No.	Category	Number of Children	Academic factor %	Economic factor %	Social Factor (%)	Total
1.	Male	23	80.8	67.7	56.8	68.5
	Female	24	81.6	67	58.5	68.7
2.	SC & ST	21	81.4	67.1	59	69.3
	MBC & BC	26	81.2	67.4	58.2	69.1
	Willing to go to school	23	81.5	66.8	57.9	68.9
3.	Non-willing to go to school	24	81.1	67.7	58	69
4.	Daily wages	26	81.6	66.9	58.1	69
	Vendors	21	80.7	68.3	57.8	69

Form table 9, mean values obtained in three different factors represents that the mean value of Academic factor fall in the range between 80 and 82, Economic factor fall in the range between 66 and 69 and social factor fall in the range between 55 and 59 in the primary level.

At the same time the table's mean values fall in the range between 68 and 70. It is understood from this that the Academic factor stood first then Economic and social factors responsible for the dropouts of children at primary level.

Table-10

Mean value of different factors responsible for dropouts in Upper Primary Level

S. No.	Category	Number of Children	Academic factor %	Economic factor %	Social Factor (%)	Total
1.	Male	26	80.8	70	51.5	67.2
	Female	27	81	69.7	55.4	68.6
2.	SC & ST	26	93.5	71.9	56.1	70.4
	MBC & BC	27	80.3	70.3	54.9	68.5
	Willing to go to school	29	81	69.8	54.6	68.8
3.	Non-willing to go to school	24	80.8	69.8	54.8	68.4
4.	Daily wages	28	80.9	69.8	55.2	68.5
	Vendors	25	81	70.5	52.2	67.7

Form table 10, mean values obtained in three different factors represents that the mean value of Academic factor fall in the range between 80 and 81, Economic factor fall in the range between 68 and 71 and social factor fall in the range between 51 and 57. At the same time, the table's mean values fell in the range between 66 and 70.

It is understood from this that the Academic factor stood first when Economic and social factors responsible for the dropouts of children at primary level.

SECTION - B

Factor – wise analysis at primary and upper primary level

This section deals with the analysis of data on the influence of Academic, Economic and Social Factors and its significance difference between them at primary and upper primary level.

Table-11

Significance of difference among the Academic, Economic and Social factors responsible for dropouts students at Primary Level

S. No.	Category	N	M	SD	T	Remarks
1.	Academic	47	105.68	2.498	97.02	SD
	Economic	47	67.26	1.062		
2.	Academic	47	105.68	2.498	60.95	SD
	Social	47	75.23	2.243		
3.	Economic	47	67.26	1.062	22.02	SD
	Social	47	75.23	2.243		

Form the table 11, obtained that, 't' score value of 97.02, 60.95 and 22.02 with df 46 are greater than the table value 1.98 and are significant at 0.05 level. Hence, it is concluded that there was a significance of difference between the influence of the Academic and Economic Factors, Academic and Social factors and Economic and Social Factors at primary level.

From the observed mean values, it shows that means values of Academic factors is more influencing for dropouts than social and Economic factors primary level. While comparing social and economic factors, social factors is significantly influencing for dropouts than Economic factors at primary level.

Table-12

Significance of difference among the Academic, Economic and Social factors responsible for dropouts students at Upper Primary Level

S. No.	Category	N	M	SD	T	Remarks
1.	Academic	53	105.17	0.606	299.49	SD
	Economic	53	69.83	0.606		
2.	Academic	53	105.17	0.606	18.7	SD
	Social	53	69.92	13.71		
3.	Economic	53	69.93	0.606	0.048	SD
	Social	53	69.92	13.71		

Form the above table it was obtained 't' score value of 2999.49 and 18.7 respected by Academic, Economic and Academic, Social factors with df 46 are greater than 1.98 and are significant of 0.05 level.

Hence, it is revealed that there was significance between the influence of the Academic and Economic Factors, Academic and Social factors at Upper Primary level.

From the observed mean values, it shows that means values of Academic factors is more influencing for dropouts than social and Economic factors at Upper Primary level. While comparing social factors Ps approximately equal to Economic factors at Upper primary level.

Section C

Analysis of Academic factors with respect to demographic variables

This section deals with the significance of difference of the mean values of Academic factors responsible for dropouts with respect to gender that is male and female, community, willing and non-wiling to go to school and nature of to work of the students at primary level and upper primary level.

Table-13

Significance of difference of mean values of Academic factors responsible for dropouts with respect to gender at Primary Level

S. No.	Category	N	M	SD	T	Remarks
1.	Male	23	105.06	3.678	1.052	NSD
2.	Female	24	106.03	1.329		

Form the above table 13, it was obtained 't' Value 1.052 is not significant is lesser than the table value 1.98 with df 46 at 0.05 level. Hence, it is interpreted there is no significant difference on the mean values of academic factors responsible for the dropouts among the male and female children at Primary level.

Form the above table 14, the obtained 't' Value 1.824 is not significant is lesser than the table value 1.98 with df 46 at 0.05 level. Hence, it is revealed there is no significant difference on the mean values of academic factors responsible for the dropouts among the male and female children at the Upper Primary level.

Table-14

Significance of difference of mean values of Academic factors responsible for dropouts with respect to gender at Upper Primary Level

S. No.	Category	N	M	SD	T	Remarks
1.	Male	26	105	0.522	1.824	NSD
2.	Female	27	105.29	0.632		

Table-15

Significance of difference of mean value of Academic factors responsible for dropouts with respect to Community at Primary Level

S. No.	Category	N	M	SD	T	Remarks
1.	SC	21	105.84	1.308	0.653	NSD
2.	MBC / BC	26	105.58	1.335		

Form the above table 15, the obtained 't' Value 0.653 which df 46 is lesser than the table value 1.98 and is not significant 0.05 level. Hence, it is revealed there is no significance difference between the influence of SC community and backward, Most Backward community at Primary Level.

Table-16

Significance of difference of mean value of Academic factors responsible for dropouts with respect to Community at Upper Primary Level

S. No.	Category	N	M	SD	T	Remarks
1.	SC	26	108.53	18.87	1.041	NSD
2.	MBC / BC	27	105.06	0.249		

Form the above table 16, the obtained 't' Value 1.041 which df 46 is lesser than the table value 1.98 and is not significant 0.05 level. Hence, it is revealed there was not significance difference between the influence of SC community and Backward, Most Backward community at Upper Primary Level.

Table-17

Significance of difference of mean value of Academic factors responsible for dropouts with respect to Willing and Non willing to go to school at Primary Level

S. No.	Category	N	M	SD	T	Remarks
1.	Willing to go School	23	105.96	1.488	1.299	NSD
2.	Non willing to go school	24	105.46	1.079		

Form the above table 17, the obtained 't' Value 1.299 with df 46 is lesser than the table value 1.98 and is not significant 0.05 level. Hence, it is understood there was not significance of difference between the influence of willing and non willing to go to school at Primary Level.

Table-18

Significance of difference of mean value of Academic factors responsible for dropouts with respect to Willing and Non willing to go to school at Upper Primary Level

S. No.	Category	N	M	SD	T	Remarks
1.	Willing to go to school	29	105.24	0.625	0.972	NSD
2.	Non willing to go to school	24	105.08	0.571		

Form the above table 18, the obtained 't' Value 0.972 with df 46 is lesser than the table value 1.98 and is not significant 0.05 level. Hence, it is revealed there was not significance of difference between the influence of willing and non willing to go to school at Upper Primary Level.

Table-19

Significance of difference of mean value of Academic factors responsible for dropouts student at Primary Level

S. No.	Category	N	M	SD	T	Remarks
1.	Daily wages	26	106.09	1.234	3.075	SD
2.	Vendors	21	104.86	1.25		

Form the above table 19, it was obtained 't' Value of 3.075 with df 46 is greater than the table value 1.98 and is significant at 0.05 level. Hence, it is concluded that there was significant difference between the influence of the daily wages and vendors at primary level. From the observed mean values it shows that mean values of daily wages activities is more influencing for dropouts than vendors at Primary Level.

Table-20

Significance of difference of mean value of Academic factors responsible for dropouts with respect to nature of to work of the students at Upper Primary Level

S. No.	Category	N	M	SD	T	Remarks
1.	Daily wages	28	105.16	0.644	2.727	SD
2.	Vendors	25	105.25	0.433		

Form the above table 20, it was revealed that the 't' Value of 2.727 with df 46 is greater than the table value 1.98 and is significant at 0.05 level. Hence, it is interpreted that there was significant difference between the influence of the daily wages and vendors at Upper Primary level. From the observed mean values it shows that mean values of Vendors is more influencing for dropouts than daily wages at Upper Primary Level.

SECTION - D

Analysis of Economic factors with respect to demographic variables at primary and upper primary level.

This section deals with the significance of difference of the mean values of Economic factors responsible for dropouts with respect to gender that is male and female, community, willing and non willing to go to school and nature of the work of the students at primary level and upper primary level.

Form the above table 21, it was obtained 't' Value 2.046 is significant is greater than the table value 1.98 at 0.05 level. Hence, it is interpreted there is no significant difference on the mean values of Economic factors responsible for the dropouts among the male and female children at Primary level.

Table-21

Significance of difference of mean value of Economic factors responsible for dropouts with respect to gender at Primary Level

S. No.	Category	N	M	SD	T	Remarks
1.	Male	23	67.65	0.967	2.046	SD
2.	Female	24	67.03	1.048		

From the above table it is observed that meal value it shows that the mean value of male is more influencing than female at primary level.

Table-22

Significance of difference of mean values of Economic factors responsible for dropouts with respect to gender at Upper Primary Level

S. No.	Category	N	M	SD	T	Remarks
1.	Male	26	69.95	0.475	1.341	NSD
2.	Female	27	69.74	0.67		

Form the above table 22, the obtained 't' Value 1.341 is not significant is lesser than the table value 1.98 with df 46 at 0.05 level. Hence, it is revealed there is no significant difference on the mean values of Economic factors responsible for the dropouts among the male and female children at the Upper Primary level.

Table-23

Significance of difference of mean value of Economic factors responsible for dropouts with respect to Community at Primary Level

S. No.	Category	N	M	SD	T	Remarks
1.	MC	21	67.11	1.071	0.871	NSD
2.	MBC / BC	26	67.38	1.041		

Form the above table 23, the obtained 't' Value 0.871 which df 46 is lesser than the table value 1.98 and is not significant 0.05 level. Hence, it is revealed that there was no significance difference between the influence of SC community and backward, Most Backward community at Primary Level.

Table-24

Significance of difference of mean value of Economic factors responsible for dropouts with respect to Community at Upper Primary Level

S. No.	Category	N	M	SD	T	Remarks
1.	SC	26	76.91	12.49	0.738	NSD
2.	MBC / BC	27	70.27	0.998		

Form the above table 24, the obtained 't' Value 0.738 which df 46 is lesser than the table value 1.98 and is not significant 0.05 level. Hence, it is interpreted that there was not significant of difference between the influence of SC community and Backward, Most Backward community at Upper Primary Level.

Table-25

Significance of difference of mean value of Economic factors responsible for dropouts with respect to willing and Non willing to go to school at Primary Level

S. No.	Category	N	M	SD	T	Remarks
1.	Willing to go to school	23	66.83	1.049	2.937	SD
2.	Non willing to go to school	24	67.67	0.898		

Form the above table 25, the obtained 't' Value 2.937 with df 46 is greater than the table value 1.98 and is not significant 0.05 level. Hence, it is understood there was not significance of difference between the influence of willing and non willing to go to school at Primary Level.

From the observed mean value it shows that the mean value of non willing to go to school is more influencing than willing to go to school at Primary level.

Form the above table 26, the obtained 't' Value 0.25 with df 46 is lesser than the table value 1.98 and is not significant 0.05 level. Hence, it is revealed there was not significance of difference between the influence of willing and non willing to go to school at Upper Primary Level.

Table-26

Significance of difference of mean value of Economic factors responsible for dropouts with respect to Willing and Non willing to go to school at Upper Primary Level

S. No.	Category	N	M	SD	T	Remarks
1.	Willing to go to school	29	69.83	0.647	0.25	NSD
2.	Non willing to go to school	24	69.79	0.553		

Table-27

Significance of difference of mean value of Economic factors responsible for dropouts with respect to nature of the work of the students at Primary Level

S. No.	Category	N	M	SD	T	Remarks
1.	Daily wages	26	66.91	1.042	5.294	SD
2.	Vendors	21	68.26	0.655		

Form the above table 27, it was obtained 't' Value of 5.294 with df 46 is greater than the table value 1.98 and is significant at 0.05 level. Hence, it is concluded that there was significant difference between the influence of the daily wages and vendors at primary level.

From the observed mean values it showed that mean values of vendors is more influencing for dropouts than daily wages at Primary Level.

Table-28

Significance of difference of mean value of Economic factors responsible for dropouts with respect to nature of to work of the students at Upper Primary Level

S. No.	Category	N	M	SD	T	Remarks
1.	Daily wages	28	69.79	0.667	2.198	SD
2.	Vendors	25	70.5	0.866		

Form the above table 28, it was obtained 't' Value of 2.198 with df 46 is greater than the table value 1.98 and is significant at 0.05 level. Hence, it is interpreted that there was significant difference the influence of daily wages and vendors at Upper Primary level. From the observed mean values it shows that mean values of Vendors is more influencing than daily wages at Upper Primary Level.

SECTION- E

Analysis of Social factors with respect to demographic variables at primary and upper primary level

This section deals with the significance of difference of the mean values of Social factors responsible for dropouts with respect to gender that is male and female, community, willing and non willing to go to school and nature of the work of the students at primary level and upper primary level.

Table-29

Significance of difference of mean value of Social factors responsible for dropouts with respect to gender at Primary Level

S. No.	Category	N	M	SD	T	Remarks
1.	Male	23	73.77	15.97	0.593	NSD
2.	Female	24	76.07	1.093		

Form the above table 29, it was obtained 't' Value 0.593 is significant is Lesser than the table value 1.98 with df 46 at 0.05 level. Hence, it is interpreted there is no significant difference on the mean values of Social factors responsible for the dropouts among the male and female children at Primary level.

Table-30

Significance of difference of mean values of Social factors responsible for dropouts with respect to gender at Upper Primary Level

S. No.	Category	N	M	SD	T	Remarks
1.	Male	26	66.95	20.798	1.141	NSD
2.	Female	27	72.03	1.926		

Form the above table 30, the obtained 't' Value 1.141 is not significant is lesser than the table value 1.98 with df 46 at 0.05 level. Hence, it is revealed there is no significant difference on the mean values of Social factors responsible for the dropouts among the male and female children at the Upper middle level.

Table-31

Significance of difference of mean value of Social factors responsible for dropouts with respect to Community at Primary Level

S. No.	Category	N	M	SD	T	Remarks
1.	MC	21	74.63	2.757	1.495	NSD
2.	MBC / BC	26	75.62	8.945		

Form the above table 31, the obtained 't' Value 1.49 which df 46 is lesser than the table value 1.98 and is not significant 0.05 level. Hence, it is revealed that there was no significance difference between the influence of SC community and backward, Most Backward community at Primary Level.

Table-32

Significance of difference of mean value of Social factors responsible for dropouts with respect to Community at Upper Primary Level

S. No.	Category	N	M	SD	T	Remarks
1.	MC	26	72.97	12.34	0.695	NSD
2.	MBC / BC	27	71.33	3.477		

Form the above table 32, the obtained 't' Value 0.695 which df 46 is lesser than the table value 1.98 and is not significant 0.05 level. Hence, it is interpreted that there was not significant of difference between the influence of SC community and Backward, Most Backward community at Upper Primary Level.

Form the above table 33, the obtained 't' Value 0.193 with df 46 is Lesser than the table value 1.98 and is not significant 0.05 level. Hence, it is understood there was not significance of difference between the influence of willing and non willing to go to school at Primary Level.

Table-33

Significance of difference of mean value of Social factors responsible for dropouts with respect to willing and Non willing to go to school at Primary Level

S. No.	Category	N	M	SD	T	Remarks
1.	Willing to go to school	23	75.30	2.544	0.193	NSD
2.	Non willing to go to school	24	75.42	1.579		

Table-34

Significance of difference of mean value of Social factors responsible for dropouts with respect to Willing and Non willing to go to school at Upper Primary Level

S. No.	Category	N	M	SD	T	Remarks
1.	Willing to go to school	29	71.03	3.189	0.214	NSD
2.	Non willing to go to school	24	71.21	2.929		

Form the above table 34, the obtained 't' Value 0.214 with df 46 is lesser than the table value 1.98 and is not significant 0.05 level. Hence, it is revealed there was not significance of difference between the influence of willing and non willing to go to school at Upper Primary Level.

Table-35

Significance of difference of mean value of Social factors responsible for dropouts with respect to nature of the work of the students at Primary Level

S. No.	Category	N	M	SD	T	Remarks
1.	Daily wages	26	75.56	1.391	1.988	SD
2.	Vendors	21	75.14	3.09		

Form the above table 35, it was obtained 't' Value of 1.988 with df 46 is greater than the table value 1.98 and is significant at 0.05 level. Hence, it is revealed that there was significant difference between the influence of the daily wages and vendors at primary level.

From the observed mean values it shows that mean values of daily wages is more influencing for dropouts than vendors at Primary Level.

Table-36

Significance of difference of mean value of Social factors responsible for dropouts with respect to nature of to work of the students at Upper Primary Level

S. No.	Category	N	M	SD	T	Remarks
1.	Daily wages	28	71.72	2.878	3.992	SD
2.	Vendors	25	67.88	2.421		

Form the above table 36, it was obtained 't' Value of 3.992 with df 46 is greater than the table value 1.98 and is significant at 0.05 level. Hence, it is interpreted that there was significant difference the influence of daily wages and vendors at Upper Primary level.

From the observed mean values it shows that mean values of daily wages is more influencing for dropouts than vendors at Upper Primary Level.

6

Findings, suggestions and conclusion

OVER VIEW

The aim of the present study was to measure the reason of dropouts among the Kulithalai Union of Primary and Upper Primary Level children towards Academic, Economic and Social factors.

The attitude of dropouts was measured through to the attitude scale consisting of 5 points such as strongly agree, agree, neutral, disagree and strongly disagree. The framed null-hypotheses were accepted of rejected based on the results derived from the analysis of Data.

This chapter presents the Findings of the study, Conclusions, Educational simplifications and suggestions for further study.

FINDINGS OF THE STUDY

The salient findings drawn from the analysis of the data under different sectors are present below.

SECTION A:

Analysis on mean values at primary level and upper primary level.

SECTION B:

Factor wise analysis at primary level and upper primary level.

SECTION C:

Analysis on Academic factors wise respect to Demographic variables.

SECTION D:

Analysis on Economic factors wise respect to Demographic variables.

SECTION E:

Analysis on Social factors wise respect to Demographic variables.

SECTION A: ANALYSIS ON MEAN VALUES

1. The mean values of Academic factors fell in the range between 80 and 82, Economic factors fell in the range between 66 and 69 and social factors fell in the range between 55 and 59 in the primary level.
   It was understand from this that Academic factor stood first and then Economic and Social factors responsible for the dropouts of children at primary level.
2. In the upper primary level, the mean values of Academic factors fell in the range between 80 and 81, Economic factors fell in the range between 68 and 71 and Social factors fell in the range between 51 and 57.

It was found that Academic factors stood first then Economic factors and Social Factors responsible for dropouts of children at upper primary level.

SECTION-B

FACTOR WISE ANALYSIS AT PRIMARY AND UPPER PRIMARY LEVEL

3. Significant difference has been observed between Academic factors, Economic Factors and Social factors. It was also found that the mean values of Academic factors were more influencing in the dropouts of primary level children.
4. Similarly in the upper primary level too, the significant difference has been observed between Academic factors, Economic factors and social factors. It was also found that the mean value of Academic factors was more influences in the dropouts of upper primary level children.
5. It was found that the significant difference between Academic factors Vs Economic factors and Academic factors Vs Social Factors in the dropouts of primary level children.
6. It was also found that the significant difference between Academic factors Vs Economic factors and Academic factors Vs Social factors But not wish Economic factors Vs Social factors in the dropouts of upper primary level children.
7. It was also found that Academic factors was more influencing than Economic factors and Social factors where as Economic factors and social factors are found to be similar.

SECTION-C

Analysis on Academic factors with respect to demographic variables at primary and upper primary level.

8. It was found that there was no significant difference on the mean values of Academic factors responsible for dropouts among the male and female children at primary level.
9. Similarly in the upper primary level, there was no significant difference on the mean values of Academic factors responsible for dropouts among the male and female children.
10. It was found that there was not significance of difference between the influence of SC Community and BC / MBC community at Primary level.

11. Similarly in the Upper Primary level, there was significance of difference between the influence of SC Community and MBC / BC community.
12. It was understood there was not significance of difference between the influence of willing and non willing to go to school at Primary level.
13. Similarly in the Upper Primary level, it was found that there was significance of difference between the influence of willing and non willing to go to school.
14. There was significance of difference between the influence of Daily wages and vendors at Primary level.

From the observed mean values it shows that mean values of dropouts engaging in Daily wages was more influencing for dropouts engaging in vendors at Primary level.

15. Similarly, in the Upper Primary level, there was significance of difference between the influence of dropouts engaging in daily wages and vendors.

From the observed mean values it shows that mean values of dropouts engaging in vendors was more influencing for dropouts than dropouts engaging in daily wages at Upper Primary level.

SECTION-D

ANALYSIS ON ECONOMIC FACTORS WITH RESPECT TO DEMOGRAPHIC VARIABLES AT PRIMARY AND UPPER PRIMARY LEVEL

16. It was found that there significant difference on the mean values of Economic factors responsible for the dropouts among the male and female children at primary level.

From the observed mean values it shows that the mean value of male was more influencing than female at primary level.

17. In the Upper Primary level; there was no significance of difference on the mean value of Economic factors responsible for the dropouts among the male and female children.
18. It was found that there was not significance of difference between the influence of SC community and MBC / BC community at Primary level.

19. Similarly, in the Upper Primary level there was significance of difference between the influence of SC Community and MBC/BC community.
20. It was understood that there was significance of difference between the influence of willing and non willing to go to school among dropouts Primary level. From the observed mean values it shows that the mean value of non willing to go to school was more influencing than willing to go to school at among dropouts primary level.
21. But in the Upper Primary level, there was not significance of difference between the influence of willing and non willing to go to school among dropouts children.
22. It was found that there was significance of difference between the influence of Daily wages and vendors at Primary level.

    From the observed mean values it shows that mean value of dropouts engaging vendors it was more influencing for dropouts than daily wages at primary level.
23. Similarly, in the Upper Primary level, there was significance of difference between the influence of dropouts engaging in daily wages and vendors. From the observed mean values it shows that the mean values of dropouts engaging in vendors was more influencing than dropouts engaging in daily wages at Upper Primary level.

SECTION-E

FACTORWISE ANALYSIS AT PRIMARY AND UPPER PRIMARY LEVEL

24. It was found that there was no significance of difference on the mean values of social factors responsible for the dropouts among the male and female children at Primary level.
25. Similarly, in the Upper Primary level it was found that there was no significance of difference on the mean values of social factors responsible for dropouts among the male and female children.
26. It was found that there was no significance of difference

between the influence of SC community and BC/ MBC community at Primary level

27. Similarly, in the Upper Primary level, It was found that there was not significance of difference between the influence of SC Community and BC/MBC community.
28. It was found that there was not significance of difference between the influence of willing and non willing to go to school at Primary level.
29. Similarly in the Upper Primary level, It was found that there was not significance of difference between the influence of willing and non willing to go to school among dropouts.
30. It was found that there was significance of difference between the influence of dropouts engaging at Daily wages and vendors at Primary level. From the observed mean values it shows that the mean value if shows that the mean value of dropouts engaging in daily wages was more influencing than dropouts engaging in vendors at primary level.
31. Similarly, in the Upper Primary level, it was found that there was significance of difference between the influence of dropouts engaging in daily wages and vendors. From the observed mean values it shows that the mean values of dropouts engaging in daily wages was more influencing than dropouts engaging in vendors at Upper Primary level.

DISCUSSION OF THE STUDY

It was understood from the perusal of the study that all the dropouts children irrespective of sex, community, willing and non willing to go to school and present their occupation were having the favourable attitude to the range of around 75 percent towards Academic, Economic, and social factors. It shows that they are having good option towards the above variables. This may be due to the fact that the students have become dropouts children not because of interest, but because of some other compulsions.

Though all the children having favourable attitude towards dropouts children, there was some difference when the analysis was made between certain variables. It was reported that positively high significant was observed among Academic and Economic factor than social factors at primary and Upper Primary level. It is inferred from the fact that students will behave normally when there are given equal education opportunities.

It was reported that positively high significant difference was observed among dropouts engaging in daily wages than dropouts engaging vendors activities at primary and Upper Primary level.

It was reported that positively high significant difference of Economic factors was observed among boys than girls at primary level. But the Primary level there was no significant difference between boys and girls.

It was reported that positively high significant difference between willing and non willing to go to school in primary level. The dropouts children at primary level willing to go to school are more than non willing to go to school. But the Upper Primary level there was no significant difference between willing and non willing to go to school.

The significant difference among the dropouts may be more educational awareness among the boys at primary level and Upper Primary level.

CONCLUSION OF THE STUDY

It is concluded from the findings that all the children are having favourable attitude towards the dropouts children. The same trend in the attitude was observed when the sample was classified with respect to sex, community, willing and non willing to go to school and wish respect to nature of the work of the dropouts children at primary and Upper Primary level. When the analysis was made between the variables it was observed that the attitudes towards "Academic factors" and "Economic factors" were more than other variables such as "Social factor".

BIBLIOGRAPHY

1. Bhatnagar, Suresh. *Indian Education Today and Tomorrow.* Meerut: Internation, 1983 pp. 124-148.

2. Bihari., L.R., (1969). Wastage and Stagnation in primary education among the tribals, Tribal Research and Training Institute, Gujarat Vidyapeeth. Ahmedabad, Buch, M.B., Third Survey of Research in Education (1978 – 83). P. 133.
3. Cervantes., L.F. *The dropouts: Causes and cures,* Ann Arbor: Michigan Press, 1965.
4. Cohen, S.B., and Betten Court, L.U. (1991). Drop-out: intervening with reluctant learner, intervention in school and clinic. In sociological Abstract. 42 (I). 1994. p.178.
5. Conger, J.J. & Peterson, C.A. *Adolescence and Youth,* Third ed. New York: Harper and Row, 1984. pp. 146, 148, 152, 425.
6. Contractor, B.M., (1977) Educational attainment as a function of certain variables. Ph.D., psy. Gujarat U., buch, M.B. Third Survey of Research in Education. (1978-83). p.661.
7. Crow, L.D. and Crow, L. *Educational Psychology.* New Delhi: Eurasia. 1962. pp. 145-146.
8. Dass, J.R and Grag, V.P. (1985): Impact of Preprimary education on dropouts, stagnation and academic performance, Education Department, Municipal Corporation, Delhi. Buch, M.B. Fourth Survey of Research in Education (1983-88). Vol.II, p.1265.
9. Das, D.C. (1969). A study of the wastage and stagnation at the elementary level of education in the state of Assam with special reference to the primary stage, SIE. Assam, Buch, M.B., Fourth Survey of research in Education (1983-88).
10. Das R.C. (1979). Effectiveness of teacher training in reducing educational wastage. SIE, Assam, Buch, M.B., Fourth survey of Research in Education (1983-88) Vol.II, p.930.
11. Das R.C. (1975). A comparative study of educational wastage in urban and rural areas. SIE, Assam, Buch, M.B., Fourth survey of Research in Education (1983-88) Vol.II, p.1263.
12. Delores, Jaques. (1996). Learning: The Treasure within. Report to UNESCO of the International Commission for the 21st century.

13. Davies, Scott (1994). In search of resistance and rebellion among high school dropouts. Canadian Journal of Sociology 19(3). 331-350. In Sociological Abstract (1995). 43 (2).

14. Devi, K.G. (1983). Problem of dropouts in primary schools of Manipur with special reference to Imphal Town (1963-1970). Ph.D.Edu.Gau, U.Buch, M.B., Fourth Survey of Research in Education (1983-88). Vol.II. P. 1267.

15. Figueira, Mc Donough, Josefina (1992). Community contex and dropouts rates school social work Arizona State Univ. Children and Youth services Review: In sociological Abstract. 41(2).

16. Flisher, A.J., and Chalton, D.O. (1995). High School dropouts in a working class south African community: selected characteristics and risk taking behaviour. Journal of Adolescent. Feb., 105-121. In sociological Abstract. 43 (5), 1995.

17. Franklin, C. and Streeter, C.L. (1995). Assessment of middle class youth at-risk to dropouts school, psychological and family correlates. *Children and Youth Services Review, 17,* 433-488.

18. Garcia de Vicens et al., (1979). Measurement of school dropouts in Argentina. Revista Paraguaya de Scoiologia, 16, 45. In Sociological Abstract. 29 (4), 1991.

19. Gogate, S.B. (1982), A critical study of the dropouts at the +2 stage (new XI & XII) in Raigad (Kolaba) District Maharashtra. Buch., M.B., Third Survey of Research in Education (1978-83).

20. Gupta, S.L., (1974). A Study of the impact of the ungraded school system on reducing school dropouts and stagnation in primary schools (1970-74). NCERT. New Delhi.

21. Hussain, M., (1982) Wastage and Stagnation in primary school of rural areas of Bhilwara District. SIERT, Rajasthan, Buch, M.B., Fourth Survey of Research in Education (1983-88) vol.II, p.1272.

22. Jordan, Will J., Lara and Mc Partland James (1996). Exploring the causes of early dropouts among race ethnic and gender groups. *Youth and Society,* 28, 62-94.

23. Joshi, N.D., (1981), Problems faced by certain tribal groups in Trivandrum District in relation to provision and use of school facilities. Dept. of Edu., Ker. U. Buch., M.B. Third survey of Research in Education (1978-83). pp. 78-83.

24. Kasen, Stephanie; Cohen Patricia and Brook, Judith S. (1998). Adolescent school experiences and dropouts, adolescent pregnancy, and young adult deviant behaviour. *Journal of Adolescent Research.* 13, 49-72. In child Development Abstract and Bibliography, 72 (2).

25. Kasinath, H.M. (1980). A critical study of the problems of wastage and stagnation in primary education in Karnataka State. Ph.D., Edu. Kar. U., Buch., M.B. Third Survey of Research in Education (1978-83) p.911.

26. Khandeker, M. (1974). A study of dropouts. TISS, Bombay, Buch., M.B., Second Survey of Research in Education (1972-73).

27. Khana, K. (1983). Preparation of reading material for girl dropouts in Delhi Slums. Ph.D., Edu, Del.U., Buch., M.B., Fourth Survey of Research in Education (1983-88). Vol. II p.597.

28. Leslie F. Hale, Ed. D., NCSP, et al., (1998). School dropouts Prevention: Information and Strategies for Educators, National Association of School Psychologists, 4340 East-West Highway, suit 402, Betehrsder MD 20814.

29. Mathur, J.S., Jain, S.P., and Rahim, C.A. (1982). Rural Youths from poverty groups, dropouts and non students: A study for four states. NIRD, Buch, M.B., Fourth Survey of Research in Education (1983-88). Vol I, p. 169.

30. Masavi, M. (1976). Wastage and stagnation in primary education in tribal areas. Tribal Research and Training Institute. Gujarat Vidyapith, Ahmedabad, Buch., M.B., Third Survey of Research in Education (1978-83). P. 154.

31. McCaul, J.Edward. *et al.* (1992) Consequences of dropping out of school: Findings from high school and beyond. *Journal of Education Research.* Washington, D.C: 1992, 85 (4), pp. 198-207.

32. Mc Neal, Ralph, Barners, Jr (1994). Dropping out of high school: individual and school variation. *Dissertation Abstracts International, The Humanities and Social Sciences,*55(6), 1524-A

33. Mc Neal, Ralph, B. Jr. (1995) Extra curricular activities and high school dropouts. Un *Sociology of Education,* 68. In Sociological Abstract 43 (3).

34. Nail., C. (1981). A Survey of dropouts and non enrolment of children in the 6-14 age group. Indian Institute of Education, Pune. Third Survey of Research in Education (1978-83). P.916.

35. National Dropouts prevention Centre at Clemson University; 205 Martin Street, Clemson, SC 29634-5111: (803) 656-2599; http\\www.dropoutprevention.org.

36. Nayal, G.S. and Nayal, S. (1989). Differential personality profiles of high school dropouts and stay-ins. *Indian Educational Review.* 24(3), 103-109. In fifth survey of Research in Education (1988-92). Vol. I, p.324.

37. Pellas, A.M., (1987). School dropouts in the united states Washington DC: Center for Education Statistics. (ERIC Document Reproduction Services N.Ed., 283119).

38. Pillai, G.V. Benjamin, J. and Mair, K.R., (1980). A study of dropouts in primary education in Kerala. State Planning Board, Government of Kerala, Trivandrum, Buch, MB. Third Survey of Research in Education (1978-83). p. 932.

39. Punalekar, S.P. (1975). School dropouts among Harijan children, causes and cure. Central Institute of Research and Training in Public Co-operation New Delhi. Buch., M.B., Third Survey of Research in Education (1978-83). p. 175.

40. Rumberger, R.W., (1983). Dropping out of High School: the influence of race, Sex and family background. *American Education Research Journal.* 20. 199-200.

41. Sarkar, B.N. (1980), A Pilot investigation on school dropouts reasons. Demography Research Unit. ISI, Calcutta. Buch., M.B., Third Survey of Research in Education (1978-83) p. 948.

42. Setharamu, A.S. and Ushadevi, M.D. (1981). School dropouts in Rural Areas a study of the dropouts in Karnataka State. Institute for Social and Economic Change. Bangalore, Buch., M.B., Third Survey of Research in Education (1978-83). p. 197.
43. Sharma, R.C. and Sapra. C.L., 1969. Wastage and Stagnation in primary and middle schools in India. NCERT, New Delhi.
44. SIE (U.P.) (1968) A study of dropouts and failures in primary classes, Allahabad, Buch, M.B., Fourth Survey of Research in Education (1983-88) vol II., P.1281.
45. Srivastava, S. and Gupta, A.P. (1980). Survey of the non-enrolled, non-attending and dropouts children of the age group (6-14) in the Ferozepore district. Dev. Samaj College of Education for Women, Ferozepore District. Dev.Samaj College of Education for Women, Ferozpore, Buch, M.B., Third Survey of Research in Education (1978-83). P.972.
46. Vathsala, S. (1981). Potential dropouts at middle school level. Ph.D., Edu. Madras U., Buch M.B., Third Survey of Research in Education (1978-83).

JOURNALS

1. Indian Journal of Social Work. Vol.22, No.4 January 1972, Working children in greater Bombay by Khandekar Mandakini and Naik, M.D.
2. Lok. Kalyan, Vol.2 No.1., Jan-1979, Poverty main cause of children's and Employment by Kusum.
3. Main Stream, June 1980, Poverty Breeding ground for child labours by Mohsini.
4. Social Welfare, Vol.23 No.8 1976, "Children are working in millions" by Seongupta.P.
5. Social Change, Vol.2., No.3 September 1972, Protection for the child by Baig Tara, A1.

3. Awareness on Health Habits of Students

1

Introduction

Education is the process by which people acquires knowledge, skills, habits, values or attitudes. It is the chief means of acquiring scent teaching the essential knowledge and skills. Human beings have tremendous potentialities. The purpose of education is to bring out such hidden potentialities. “Therefore bring out such hidden potentialities from individuals is a primary purpose of teaching”. Education is very closely linked with solving social problems such as improvement in the state of health. Population control and the erablication of poverty, thus constituting a major contributing factors to a country’s social economic development, and as such it represents one of the most important in international cooperation.

A quality education is custom design that addresses the unique abilities of each student and has a positive emotional experience. Custom education evaluates natural talent and how the student learns. This is why home schooled students parents learn what works and does not work then focus on what works with this method. Students develop above to learn and learning becomes a lifelong process.

Therefore, the investigator went through the surveys of educational research and educational journals available and prepared an abstract of review that is being presented in the succeeding paragraph.

HEALTH EDUCATION

Education for health beings with people. It hopes to motivate them with whatever interests they may have in improving their living conditions. It aims is to develop in them a sense of responsibility for health conditions for themselves as individuals, as members of families, and as communities. In communicable disease control, health education commonly includes an appraisal of what is known by a population about a disease, an assessment of habits and attitudes of the people as they related to spread and frequency of the disease, and the presentation of specific means to remedy observed deficiencies.

Health education is also an effective tool that helps improve health habits in developing nations. It not only teaches prevention and basic health knowledge but also conditions ideas that re-shape everyday habits of people with unhealthy lifestyles in developing countries. This type of conditioning not only affects the immediate recipients of such education but also future generations will benefit from an improved and properly cultivated ideas about health that will eventually be ingrained with widely spread health education. Moreover, besides physically health prevention, health education can also provide more aid and help people deal healthier with situations of extreme stress, anxiety, depressions or other emotional disturbances to lessen the impact of these sorts of mental and emotional constituents, which can consequently lead to detrimental physical effects.

He who enjoys good health is rich, though he knows it or not. – Italian Proverb. Human beings are born to lead a happy life. In bringing up the children, the school plays a unique role in everyone's life. A feeling of total well-being plays a critical part in attaining any lasting success or happiness in life. To achieve this state of well being, one must attain a level of fitness, which enables one to perform the best at all times. The present generation is living with a lot of distractions. They do not know how to lead a healthy life.

The term Health is defined as the state of complete physical, mental and social well-being and not merely the absence of disease and infirmity World Health Organization (WHO). The term Education is defined as by education I mean an all round drawing out of the best in the child and the man, body, mind and spirit (Gandhiji). So Health education is a combination of planned social actions and learning experiences, designed to enable people to gain control over the determinates of health and health behaviors and the conditions that affect their health status and the health status of others.

Health for all has served as an importance focal point for health strategy for WHO and its member states for almost twenty years. Although it has been interpreted differently by each country in the light of its social and economic characteristics, the health status and morbidity patterns of its population, and the state of development of its health system, it has provided an inspirational goal, based on the concept of equity of health. The Health for All Strategy is currently being redeveloped to ensure its continued relevance into the next century. A new policy is being developed, to be adopted by the World Health Assembly in 1998.

Health Education plays a crucial role in the development of a healthy, inclusive and equitable social, psychological, and physical environment. It has undergone radical change in recent years, and modern approaches now use an empowering, multi-dimensional, multi – professional approach which relates to all settings, organizations. This leading edge journal reflects the best of modern thinking about health education, offers stimulating and incisive debates, concerns, interventions and initiatives, and provides a wealth of evidence, research, information, and ideas to inform and inspire those in both the theory and practice of Health Education.

From the above Health Education the investigator had chosen only Health Habits for her research.

The health education can be impacted through physical education because students understand the relation between physical education and health education. Health Education includes,

(1) Health Habits

(2) Sports

(3) Games

(4) Yoga

HEALTH HABITS

Eating nutrition's food making the environment neatly. Free from diseases and planning for health services.

Living a healthy life is like any other thing we want to do, it is as good as we make it. Everybody wants to feel good, be happy have long life with minimal pain and discomfort. Well the absolute truth is that most of us can. Sure there are special cases of some illness or condition but in general most of us can feel better by living better.

There is a price we have to pay if we are to feel better. We need certain things to maintain our body's internal balance. We need exercise, without this our circulatory and respiratory systems don't get the work out they need and they become weak.

Our whole body suffers and we pile on layer after layer of fat when we don't get enough physical activity but what about food? What we eat, how we eat it and for some when we eat it are all very important. What and how we eat is especially important. Our body requires a balance of various foods and too long out of balance equals not feeling so good.

While there are many sources that try to tell us exactly what our body needs and in one proportion it is hard to believe that every human body requires the same. While it is not too hard to find your happy balance that place where the amount of activity and the foods you eat make you feel good.

The amount of food you consume, what types of foods and in what proportions are a matter of knowing your body. You know if coffee makes you feel yuck and if you don't know it's easy to find out, just change the amount you drink. You can just start with recommended portions and eating patterns then make small changes to see where it takes you.

Even is great health is something you are going to have to work up to you can feel better right away. Good health is as much a matter of mental, emotional and some would say spiritual balance as well as the physical. Just starting on a path to improved health is enough to feel better and encourage you to stick with it.

Eating breakfast appears to enhance alertness, attention, and performance on standardized achievement tests, report.

Sleep is vital to good health and to mental and emotional well-being. The reports that people who don't get enough slumber are more likely than others to develop psychiatric problems and to use health care services. Plus, sleep deprivation can negatively affect memory, learning, and logical reasoning.

DEFINITION OF THE OPERATION TERMS

AWARENESS

Paraphrasing Webster's collegiate dictionary. Awareness implies vigilance is observing something implies vigilance in observing something or experience and alertness in drawing inferences from what one observes.

Awareness in a personal development sense is a consciousness of which you are being and the impact that you are having on others. Heighten your awareness by imagining a small creature on your shoulder who watches over what you think and what you do and whispers what he observes in your ear.

HEALTH HABIT

Health habit means keeping the surrounding clean. Take bathing twice a day, brushing two times, washing the hands and mouth before and after eating, wear the clean dress, cutting the nail properly, combing the hair, avoid the uncleaned food items and unboiled items.

SCHOOL HEALTH EDUCATION

Providing instruction to the students about personal hygiene

Personal hygiene or cleanliness of all the parts of body is another significant way to keep the body in perfect trim. It is important for man to attend to the following points with respect to personal hygiene.

Personal Hygiene

Personal Hygiene means the cleanliness of the body. This helps a man to protect himself against any sort of ailment. We must clean our skin carefully and regularly: human skin cover, the tissue and muscles in the human body. These are two layers in human skin – one upper and other lower. In the lower layer there are numerous sweat glands. In the upper layer there are pores. Perspiration is produced by the lower layer. And it is secreted by the upper layer through the pores. If this is not properly cleaned daily with soap and sufficient water, the pores in the human skin are likely to be closed and the dirty elements in the body cannot find an outlet. This is sure to lead to so many skin diseases as well as ailments.

Cleanliness of Hair

Cleanliness of Hair is equally an important part of the personal hygiene. We must wash our hair carefully with sufficient water, dry them up, and comb them for a few minutes daily. We must also use separate brush or comb, towel and other things in cleaning our hair. This is required so that diseases are not communicated.

Cleanliness of Hands

Hands come in touch with all sorts of germs here and there, when we are handling things or shaking hands with other individuals. We must clean our hands many times a day, particularly when we are going to eat something, with some disinfection agent such as soap. We must not allow our nails to grow, for a good deal of debris or germs get accumulated in them.

Some people have bad habits of nibbling their nails or hands. This should be avoided.

Care of Eyes

Eyes are the most important part of human body and deserve to be most properly looked after. We must wash our eyes occasionally with boric acid, but daily when taking bath we should spray cold water on them. Eye-wash should be done with an eye-washer. There is no harm if we use some eye-drops as well. Some eye exercises should be done. We should also relax our eyes. Reading should be done in proper light. It should come from the left side. We should not rub eyes, when some foreign body enters the eyes, or we should not try to remove it with finger.

Care of Teeth

Care of teeth is also very important to keep the body in prefect trim. We must clean our teeth at least twice a day once in the early morning and once before going to sleep, so that no crumbs of the food that we have taken remain stuck to them. Otherwise some germs grow in teeth and they enter our body when we eat something. Whenever some trouble develops in our teeth, we should not ignore it and immediately consult some dentist for the same.

IMPORTANCE OF HEALTH HABITS

Health habit is teaching pupils an art of living. It is a process, which affects changes in the health practices of pupils and in the knowledge and attitudes related to such changes.

KNOWLEDGE OF HEALTH IS NOT HEALTH EDUCATION

Health habits do not imply taking the knowledge of health through the programme of health education. One must also practice it all the times. Our health depends on what we do, not on what we know.

JUST KNOWING, THINKING AND WISHING DOES NOT PROVIDE HEALTH HABITS

Most of us are born with a sound body and mind which must be maintained by healthy living, by practicing safe and sound health habits every day, and by doing the things that built and maintain a healthy body and mind. Just knowing, thinking and wishing does not bring health.

USING SCIENTIFIC KNOWLEDGE IS HEALTH HABITS

Using scientific knowledge to plan and act will bring maximum health to the individual, family and community. For example, the mother who boils drinking water may save the lives of her children who otherwise may die due to cholera, dysentery or typhoid.

HEALTH HABITS IMPARTS PRINCIPLES OF HYGIENE

Health habits are closely connected with the imparting of knowledge to the people about the principles of hygiene. The word Hygiene has its root in Greek word Hyginos, which means healthful. With the help of health education, students are able to acquire and practice the knowledge of various principles of hygiene in their daily life.

DEFINITION OF HEALTH EDUCATION

Dr. Thomas Wood: "Health education is the sum of experience with favorable habits, attitudes and knowledge relating to individual, community and social health"

Anthey Cuterill: "Hygiene is very roughly the process of making things difficult for germs.

SCOPE OF HEALTH HABITS

A person's health habits, attitudes and goals are the result of his learning and experiences. They are established first from what he is taught and what he sees the family doing in the home, then from imitating the habits of friends in the village, in the school and at work. The scope of health habits, which includes the following points:

i) Knowledge about growth and development.

ii) Knowledge about good food items and their contribution to the proper growth and development of the human body.

iii) Knowledge about the significance of pure and clean water, fresh air, proper rest, physical exercise recreation, amusement and sound sleep.

iv) Knowledge about the causes and cares of various diseases, ailments, injuries and arrangements for their prevention or check like mass inoculation and first aid.

v) Knowledge about the health standard of the people living in different countries of the world.

vi) Avoidance of evil habits like smoking, drinking, taking drugs and their evil effects on health. It includes physical and mental damages caused to these individuals as well as the society.

vii) Abnormal conditions and their adverse effect on health. It also includes bad habits and their evil influences on the physical and mental health of the individual.

viii) To import mass-scale information about mental health and sex hygiene in order to ensure healthy bodies and healthy minds.

ix) To provide knowledge about different diseases, their prevention and control.

x) Knowledge about recreation, rest, sleep and exercise.

AIMS AND OBJECTIVES OF HEALTH HABITS IN SCHOOL

The function of education is to prepare us for complete living. Complete living involves the right ruling of conduct in all directions under all circumstances. In what way to treat the body; in what way bring up a family: in what way to behave as a citizen: in what way to utilize all those sources of happiness which nature supplies how to use all our faculties to the greatest advantages of ourselves and others and how to live completely.

So far we discussed some of the important aims and objectives of health education in general. The specific aims and objectives of health habits at different stages are,

Primary Stage

- o To make pupils realize the value and its personal and social importance.
- o To inculcate healthy habits of living regarding personal hygiene, food, clothing and posture.

Secondary Stage

- o To help students know how they can save themselves from accidents and from the carriers of diseases, like files, mosquitoes, rats, dirt, discharge as well as polluted air, water and food.
- o To make pupils realize the value of health and its personal and social importance.
- o To inculcate habits of healthy living regarding personal hygiene food, clothing and posture.

As discussed above health is the quality of mental, physical and emotional well-being. A healthy person can lead his life effectively and comfortably and prove himself to be a very useful member of society. With the following aims and objectives the health habits programme should be introduced in the modern seats of learning.

i) To help the students to understand health problems. To solve these problems they should determine their own roles and take help from other medical agencies.

ii) To look after the purity of food and drink produced and sold in the country.

iii) To give information and education to the people about health and hygiene.

iv) To look after the sanitation and cleanliness of the place.

v) To prevent and fight diseases and infections.

vi) To arrange periodical health examination of the people and attend those who need special attention.

According to World Health Organization (WHO) Technical Report (1954) the objectives of health education are as follows:

1) To ensure that health is valued as an asset in the community.
2) To equip the people with skills, knowledge and attitudes to enable them solve their health problems by their own actions and efforts, and
3) To promote the development and proper use of health services.

PREVENTIVE MEASURES

Smallpox, diphtheria, whooping cough, typhoid, cholera, plague, tetanus and malaria can all be prevented by medicines or inculation or vaccination.

Many other diseases can be controlled by specific treatment after the child has been attacked or early symptoms have appeared. Many diseases can be prevented by keeping the child's environment clean and free from infection. Many diseases are spread through unclean water, infected milk or food stuffs. It is, therefore, necessary to boil drinking water and strain it through clean muslin cloth. Milk also should be carefully boiled. Food should be properly cooked. All raw foods should be washed carefully. All food should be kept covered, to prevent flies, carriers of disease, from sitting on it. Malaria is caused by mosquitoes. Mosquitonets must be used. Water puddles must be prevented from forming and insecticide should be used to kill the mosquitoes.

Latrines should be kept clean and properly covered. Children should be kept away as far as possible from the sick and the ailing, especially if they have T.B. or some other infectious or contagious disease.

Children should not be allowed to mix with other children when they suffer from any illness. A sick child should be kept in bed. If he has an infection disease, he should be isolated from others for a specific period and all the clothes and vessels used by him must be washed separately. His body waste should be disposed of carefully.

It is a mistake to think that common childhood diseases are mild and that every child must go through the course of these diseases. Quite often they have very serious after-effected and result in depth or physical handicaps. Some diseases are considered a personification of a particular. Goddess or they are considered a result of God's wrath. Parents should, however realize how diseases are caused and how they can be prevented.

RESPONSIBILITIES OF HOME

The man learns good and bad traits, to work with and respect people to take care of his family and do his duty to the community. An ideal home provides a healthy environment for its members leading to their sound personality development. It satisfies the basic human needs like social, emotional and physical. A child is sure to be a happy and balanced being if he is brought up in a wholesome atmosphere where there are no conflicts and quarrels.

RESPONSIBILITIES OF HOME IN RESPECT OF HEALTH HABIT

- Teach the child to keep clean
  - a) Wash his hands before and after meals and after going to the toilet.
  - b) Bath regularly.
  - c) Clean his teeth every morning and night and after each meal.
  - d) Have regular bowel movements.
  - e) Drink plenty of water to clear out his system.
- Teach him to cough and sneeze in a handkerchief or a clean piece of cloth. Tell him not to put fingers in the nose, wipe them on the walls or on his clothes.
- Teach him not to spit anywhere and everywhere.
- Teach him to use the latrine and not use the front or backyard for either urinating or passing his bowel movements.
- Teach him not to eat food bought from street vendor.
- Teach him not to play on the ground when he has no clothes on. Teach him to wash after he comes from play.

Responsibilities of community

Effective living in society implies that the individual makes a contribution to society. This means that he is working for a cause greater than himself. Improving community health and safety are some of these great causes. They too are public functions. No longer is it thought that professional groups, such as physicians, dentists, educators, engineers and others, alone can give health and safety to the public. Just as the individual earns his health status by the way he uses his innate capacities and participates in life activities, so does the public, through its individual and cooperative effort, assist in determining the health and safety of the community.

Responsibilities of the school

School health education programme can be thought of as a process by which the pupils learn to promote and protect their own health and that of the community in which they live. We know education encompasses many forms and takes place in many different situations. It may be assumed that the competencies and skills associated with health education also will be gained in many ways.

The purpose of the school imposes a considerable responsibility on health education. When one learns the skills, knowledge and standards of his society his behavior is modified or strengthened. His behaviour is modified relative to the standards of his society.

Motivation through good instruction

School should make the programmes of Health and Education Compulsory. The programme in health and physical education should be compulsory, for the people who need it most are not the most likely to volunteer. At the outset they will not have good coordination and will not do physical things well. They fell embarrassed and won't want to participate, but we must remember that these children will functions as adults as well as their health and physical vigour permit. If education does not condition people for the world they will actually be involved in, it has failed to meet its responsibilities. School board members and educators should take a realistic look at the curriculum in health and physical education, recognizing the basic fundamental importance of quality instruction that will be motivating the future living habits of students.

To orient the students about health hABITS

To look after one's health carefully, one should follow the following six rules of health:

- o The boy must be provided with balanced and nutritious diet.
- o Fresh air and light be provided.
- o We should protect our body against the severity of extreme cold and hot.
- o Adequate exercise and adequate relaxation.
- o Protect ourselves against germs and diseases.
- o Regeneration of one's time and activities.

TO ORIENT THE STUDENTS ABOUT HABITS OF LONGEVITY

In order to live longer, we should also follow the following habits of longevity

a) Residential quarters should be open and airy.

b) We should spend most of our time in the open and for that we should prefer to adopt such professions as may enable us to do so.

c) We should prefer to sleep in the open if possible, depending upon the time, season and present condition of health.

d) We should acquire the habit of deep breathing.

e) We should never indulge in over-eating or eat more than what may be required.

f) Meat and spices should not be taken in excess.

g) We should avoid tension, worry, etc.

h) We should eat less and chew more.

i) We should ride less and walk more.

j) We should talk less and think more.

k) We should ease ourselves daily.

l) We should sit, stand and walk straight.

m) We should clean out mouth, teeth and tongue daily.

n) We should take exercise daily.

o) We should protect ourselves against all infections and germs.

p) We must clean our hands before we eat anything.
q) We should have a fixed time for eating.
r) We must work according to capacity and never be strained.
s) We should lead a normal life.
t) We must have good working knowledge of rules of health hygiene and physiology.

STATEMENT OF THE PROBLEM

The present study is entitled *"AWARENESS ON HEALTH HABITS AMONG HIGH SCHOOL STUDENTS IN PENNAKARAM BLOCK"*.

NEED OF STUDY

- Most people in our society are still unconcerned and ignorant on the issue of Health Habits. The student teacher are the guardian of our future generations and they are going to be the architects of our society. There is a need to bring out awareness among the future teacher on what is Health Habit? How is affect our life, our economic prosperity and Health and other welfare. How all of us together can save the Health for the benefit of present and future generations and achieve the ultimate objective of stabilizing the atmosphere by way of bringing awareness among the children.
- It is everyone responsibility to educate, sensitize and train the future citizens of the world on the issue of Health Habits and Health Education. Possibility of advancing in the right direction in the controlling of Health Education is possible if the endurable and responsible effort of the student teacher and teacher are channeled sensibly by providing the knowledge of Health Habits to pupils. The teachers and the student teachers can do if they themselves are aware of the problem and consequence of Health education and Health Habits.

OBJECTIVES OF THE STUDY

1) To find out the level of awareness on Health Habits among high school students.

2) To find out the level of significant difference on the awareness of Health Habits between boys and girls high school students.
3) To find out the level of significant difference on the awareness of Health Habits between hosteller's and day scholars high school students.
4) To find out the level of significant difference on the awareness of Health Habits between government and matriculation schools.
5) To find out the level of significant difference on the awareness of Health Habits between rural and urban.
6) To find out the level of significant difference on the awareness of Health Habits between educated and uneducated parents.
7) To find out the level of significant difference on the awareness of Health Habits between the parents profession.

HYPOTHESES OF THE STUDY

1) There is no significant difference between boys and girls high school students on the awareness of Health Habits.
2) There is no significant difference between hosteller's and day scholars high school students on the awareness of Health Habits.
3) There is no significant difference between government and matriculation high school students on the awareness of Health Habits.
4) There is no significant difference between urban and rural high school students on the awareness of Health Habits.
5) There is no significant difference between educated and uneducated parents children on the awareness of Health Habits among high school students.
6) There is no significant difference on the awareness of Health Habits between the parents profession among high school students.

DELIMITATIONS OF THE STUDY

Broadly speaking any study is impossible without limitation. Researcher studies in general will have limitation due to many factors. This study too has some limitations. It is responsibility of the researcher to see that the study is conducted with maximum care in order to be reliable. However, the following limitations were unavoidable in the present study.

i) The investigator was unable to investigate all the high schools students. Few schools were selected in investigate on it. The study was confined to only five schools in pennakaram block.
ii) In those schools male and female students were only taken for this study.
iii) In this present study the investigator analyzed about the awareness of the variables such as literate and illiterate parents, residence, medium and locality.

In spite of the above mentioned limitations. Sufficient care has been taken in selecting the sample, constructing the tool, gathering reliable data and applying appropriate statistical analysis etc.,

ORGANIZATION OF THE STUDY

The report of the thesis will be presented according to the following sequences.

i. The first chapter gives introduction, definition of terms, statement of problem, objectives of the study, hypotheses of the study, limitation of the study.
ii. Second chapter deals with the review of related literature which are done in India and abroad related to the study.
iii. Third chapter gives a detailed account of research procedures and methodology which includes tool, samples, administration of the tool and collection of the data.
iv. Fourth chapter deals with analysis and interpretation of the data. The results are given by applying appropriate statistical techniques. Necessary tables and graphical representation are included here.
v. The fifth chapter describes the findings, conclusion and certain recommendations about the study.

This is followed by the bibliography and appendices which consist of the tools used for the study and the related matters.

CONCLUSION

In this chapter Health Education, Health Habits, School Health Education, Importance of Health Habits, Scope of Health Habits, Aims and Objectives of Health Habits in School Responsibilities of home and School. The next chapter, deals with Review of Related literature studies.

2

Review of Related Literature

INTRODUCTION

"A Good thesis is over that me how to replicate or extend the previous work with improvement to reduce bias eliminate flows, consider pertinent variables, settle unsolved issued to check contradictory or uncertain in findings".

The aim of this chapter is to record briefly a survey of literature related to the problems under study. It is necessary to enter on any research project. This will help in understanding the several of the problem.

The research worker must be acquainted with up-to-date information about what has been thought and done in the specific area from which he intends to take up a problem of research.

A review of related literature gives the scholar an understanding of the previous work that has been done in the area. It enables him to know the means of getting to the frontlet in the field of his problems methods and limitations and it enable him to locate compensative data useful in the interpretation of results.

PURPOSE OF REVIEW LITERATURE

The following are the same of the purpose of literature:

- o It provides ideas, theories, explanations or hypotheses valuable in formulation the problem.
- o To avoid the risk of duplicating some of the studies already undertaken.
- o To suggest methods or research methodologies appropriate to the problem.
- o It widens the horizon of the researcher.
- o It suggest valuable basis for hypothesis.
- o It helps delimit the problems.
- o It help the investigator not to allow the mistake or 100 phones or pitfall which occurred in the previous findings.
- o To locate compensative data useful in the interpretation of results.
- o It contributed to the investigator for the general scholarship.

According to Best (1977) "familiarity with the literature in any problem area helps the student to discover what is already known, what others have attempted to find out, what methods of attacks have been promising or disappointing and what problem remain to be solved"

Mouly (1984) says "survey of related literature avoids the risk of duplication provide theories, ideas, explanations or hypothesis valuable in formulating the problem and contributing to the general scholarship of the investigator".

The review of literature is a necessity for any research for the following reasons.

- o It enables the investigator to study the work done earlier (previously) in the area of research.

REVIEWS FROM ABROAD

Donna B. Johnson (2003) Healthy Habits Washington WIC Program - WIC offers a unique mechanism to respond to the increasing prevalence of lifestyle-related diseases in low-income families. The Healthy Habits project was developed to augment the tools available to Welfare and Institutions Code (WIC) in its efforts to promote healthy lifestyles. The purpose of Healthy Habits was to provide training, materials and support to local WIC staff so that staff could more effectively promote healthy behaviors in WIC families and in their communities. The goals of Healthy Habits were to: 1)Increase local WIC staff expertise and ability to provide effective participant-centered, behavioral approaches to nutrition services. 2) Increase local WIC capacity to apply public health approaches to develop and sustain community-based nutrition services and chronic disease risk reduction. Healthy Habits had two components: 1) Newly developed nutrition education modules for use by local agencies and community partners to promote family meals or family physical activity; and 2) A program of mini-grants awarded to local agencies to support integration of the newly developed modules and other innovative approaches into their programs. The project incorporated theoretical approaches from social ecological models, social marketing, and Stages of Change, and included a strong focus on evaluation. Surveys and focus groups of WIC participants and staff also provided valuable information used in component design. In a six-month implementation period, use of the Healthy Habits modules was associated with staff and participant behavior change. WIC families learned new ways to be physically active together and how to incorporate family meals into their lives.

Shin-ya Kaneko et al, (2004) Health Habits of Female Shift Workers - this paper examines the effects of shift work on the lifestyles of female factory workers. As an indicator of healthy lifestyle habits, we used a scoring system based on Lester Breslow's health habits. The health scores of the women was higher than that of the non-shift workers ($p<0.01$). In addition, the score of workers who had changed from non-shift work to double-shift work was remarkably low ($p<0.01$). These results suggests that, while the female shift workers manage to maintain relatively healthy lifestyles in comparison with the males, they have more difficulty maintaining these habits than do female workers who do not perform shift work. It can be concluded that, in addition to heightening women's consciousness of their own health, surrounding entities such as the work environment, the home, and the community in general need to pay due care to Japan's female shift workers.

Margie Ford Williams (2005) The Relationship between Health Habits and Health Interests of Students and Employees in a Nontraditional University-*This study investigated the health interests of students and full-time employees of a small, nontraditional university, and examined the relationships between selected health habits and correlated health interests. Health habits were assessed using the Wellness Check for Adults developed by the Rhode Island Health Department, and interest in health promotion programs was ascertained by the Health Interests Survey modified by the investigator. Significant* ($p < .05$) *differences between students and employees were found in their interest in 5 of the 11 health promotion programs listed. Responses to ranking 3 programs of most interest revealed that for students, exercising, weight control, and nutrition were prioritized, whereas employees ranked managing stress, nutrition, and weight control. Results of bivariate analyses (Mann-Whitney U) relating health habits to specific health interests varied in direction of association and in significance. The results suggest a need to ask potential participants what health promotion programming they would be interested in attending rather than developing programs based only on identified health risk behaviors. Implications for further research are addressed.*

Japanese Health Science Center at Jikei University in **2006,** the diagnostic criteria for Japan-specific metabolic syndrome were published. The representative health habits are Breslow's seven healthy practices, Morimoto's eight items and Ikeda's six healthy habits. We investigated the prevalence of metabolic syndrome related with life-style strongly among these three sets of healthy habit. Cross-sectional study was conducted for the prevalence of metabolic syndrome by practicing these healthy habits. 20,776 Japanese individuals visited the Health Science Center at Jikei University Hospital in Japan for medical check-ups. Subjects were divided into 8 groups based on gender and age (females in their

30s, 40s, 50s and 60s, and males in their 30s, 40s, 50s and 60s). Participants completed a simple, self-administered lifestyle questionnaire based on the three sets of healthy habits. Subjects were divided into three groups (poor, moderate and favorable) according to each of the healthy habit criteria. Significant differences were observed among 10 groups for Breslow's seven healthy practices, 4 groups for Morimoto's eight items, and 13 groups for Ikeda's six healthy habits. Ikeda's six healthy habits showed the most significant differences among the three sets of habits. Among the three methods tested, to practice more Ikeda's healthy habits were the most useful for metabolic syndrome.

John C Barefoot, Morten Grønbæk, John R Feaganes, R Sue McPherson, Redford B Williams and Ilene C Siegler (2007) Alcoholic beverage preference, diet, and health habits in the University of North Carolina (UNC) Alumni Heart Study - Moderate alcohol intake is related to better health, and additional benefits may be associated with wine. However, beverage preference may be confounded by lifestyle factors related to health. The goal was to describe the associations between alcoholic-beverage preferences and indicators of a healthy diet and other health habits. This cross-sectional study included data from 2864 men and 1571 women enrolled in the UNC Alumni Heart Study. Self-reports of drinking habits were used as predictors of health behaviors and of intakes of nutrients and food groups. Subjects who preferred wine had healthier diets than did those who preferred beer or spirits or had no preference. Wine drinkers reported eating more servings of fruit and vegetables and fewer servings of red or fried meats. The diets of wine drinkers contained less cholesterol, saturated fat, and alcohol and more fiber. Wine drinkers were less likely to smoke. Compared with all drinkers, those who drank no alcohol consumed fewer vegetables but more fiber. Nondrinkers were less likely to exercise regularly and had a higher mean body mass index. Controlling for income and education had little effect on these associations. The apparent health benefits of wine compared with other alcoholic beverages, as described by others, may be a result of confounding by dietary habits and other lifestyle factors. Confounding by lifestyle variables could also be a factor in the previously observed health differences between drinkers and nondrinkers, although the evidence for this association is not as strong.

J A Ballweg and L Li (2008) Comparison of health habits of military personnel with civilian populations. The relationship between health habits and health status has gained attention in the literature in recent decades. In this report, the health habits of a particular occupational group—the military—are compared with those of the civilian population, and the extent to which the health habits of the military personnel are associated with their health status is examined. Responses to two surveys conducted in 1985 were analyzed by age group, sex, race, and educational level. The comparisons involved six of the seven health habits included in the Alameda study. Military personnel, because they are younger and their lives are more regimented, excel in meeting weight standards for the services and engaging in desirable levels of physical activity. Smoking habits of military personnel were less favorable than those of the civilians. An examination of the health status of the military for the year preceding the survey suggested that some health habits have immediate manifestations, but the impact of others may not be evident until later in life.

P Lally, A Chipperfield and J Wardle (2009) Healthy habits: efficacy of simple advice on weight control based on a habit-formation model - to evaluate the efficacy of a simple weight loss intervention, based on principles of habit formation. An exploratory trial in which overweight and obese adults were randomized either to a habit-based intervention condition (with two subgroups given weekly vs. monthly weighing; *n*=33, *n*=36) or to a waiting-list control condition (*n*=35) over 8 weeks. Intervention participants were followed up for 8 months. A total of 104 adults (35 men, 69 women) with an average BMI of 30.9 kg m"2. Intervention participants were given a leaflet containing advice on habit formation and simple recommendations for eating and activity behaviours promoting negative energy balance, together with a self-monitoring checklist. Weight change over 8 weeks in the intervention condition compared with the control condition and weight loss maintenance over 32 weeks in the intervention condition. At 8 weeks, people in the intervention condition had lost significantly more weight (mean=2.0 kg) than those in the control condition (0.4kg), with no difference between weekly and monthly weighing subgroups. At 32 weeks, those who remained in the study had lost an average of 3.8 kg, with 54% losing 5% or more of their body weight. An intention-to-treat analysis (based on last-observation-carried-forward) reduced this to 2.6 kg, with 26% achieving a 5% weight loss. This easily disseminable, low-cost, simple intervention produced clinically significant weight loss. In limited resource settings it has potential as a tool for obesity management.

Eva Vidali-Laloumi (2010) Án Innovative Preschool Health Education Program - The aim of the present study was to explore the effects of health education program, related to the identification of healthy and unhealthy nutritional habits, physical activities and hygiene in children 4-5 years of age. Method and material: 125 children participated in an education program for a period of two months. For data collection, a specialized protocol was constructed with pictures in order to evaluate the children's knowledge about healthy behavior before and after the implementation of the education program. The results of the present study showed that after the implementation of the program the scores were higher in identifying healthy and unhealthy nutritional habits and physical activities compared to the scores before the program, with statistical significant difference, p=<0,001. In regard to the place of residence, children from downgraded areas presented higher performance than children from privileged areas in identifying healthy and unhealthy physical activities and hygiene, with statistical significant difference, p=<0,005.

From the results of the present study it becomes obvious that taking up habits of healthy nutrition, exercise and hygiene constitutes the main requirement for the child's healthy development and a guarantee for a healthy adulthood. Despite the limitations of research ours findings suggests that health education programs based on motor activities and games can be successful for teaching healthy habits to preschoolers.

REVIEWS FROM INDIA

Antara Dhargupta, Minati Sen (2001) Relative Deprivation, Poor Health Habits and Mortality Using individual-level data on males from the 1988-1991 National Health Interview Survey Multiple Causes of Death Files, we examine the impact of relative deprivation within a reference group on health. We use measures of relative deprivation based on Yitzhaki's index and define reference groups using combinations of state, race, education, and age, and. Those with high relative deprivation have a higher probability of death, are more likely to self-report poor health, have high blood pressure or disabilities, and have a host of poor health habits including smoking, not wearing safety belts, high body mass index and not exercising.

Simpson WF, Brehm HN, Rasmussen ML, Ramsay J, Probst JC. (2002) Health and Fitness Profiles Of Collegiate Undergraduate Students. One goal of Healthy People: 2000 (HP:2000) and HP:2010 is to assist Americans to live healthier and improve quality of life. College students represent future consumers of health care services. Preventive measures and habits formed as young adults may have an impact on health care delivery in the 21st century. The purpose of this investigation was to compare the health habits/fitness profiles from two cohorts of undergraduate students. During the spring semesters of 1994 (SP94) and 1996 (SP96) a total of 428 male and 460 female underclass students enrolled in a general wellness class. A physical fitness assessment and a health/exercise survey were administered. Students fell within normal limits (WNL) for height, weight, BMI and percent fat. VO_2max estimated from a cycle ergometer test revealed average fitness levels. Subjects reported less than 3 days/week were spent participating in aerobic activities. Males responded spending 2.2 days/week resistance training and females 0.9 days/week. A decrease in organized physical activity after high school was reported. Overall, >75% males and >67% females reported drinking alcohol. Males consumed >15 drinks/week and females >5 drinks/week with beer being the choice drink. Thursdays-Saturdays were the common nights for consumption. Cigarette smoking for both genders in SP94 was 13% with males reported 12% and females 17% in SP96. Marijuana use during SP94 was 27% and 16% increasing to 57% and 34% for males and females receptively. These college student's fitness categories and body composition were within normal limits. However, self-reports of exercise were below HP:2000 objectives. Alcohol consumption and marijuana smoking exceeded expected goals. Women reported an increase in cigarette smoking in SP96. These data suggest that the trend for these young adults towards unhealthy health practices is present at the studied university. The need for preventative education programs to prevent these habits is essential if the Healthy People goals are to be met.

Ball, Susan, Bax (2003) *Self-care in Medical Education: Effectiveness of Health-habits Interventions for First-year Medical Students - To examine changes in health habits (sleep, alcohol, and exercise) and the effects of an educational intervention promoting self-care on the emotional and academic adjustment of first-year medical students. Fifty-four medical students completed questionnaires that assessed various health habits, alcohol use, depression severity, and areas of life satisfaction at the beginning of the semester, at mid-term, and at finals. Approximately half of the students received written feedback or participated in an educational discussion group at mid-term. The students demonstrated significant changes in health habits, with increases in alcohol consumption and decreases in exercise and socialization. The changes in health habits were predictive of both emotional and academic adjustment, with students who decreased in positive health habits, particularly socialization, being more depressed at finals. The feedback and educational interventions influenced some sleep and exercise behaviors, but the groups did not differ in overall emotional or academic adjustment. First-year medical students show significant changes in health habits as they adjust to medical school. An educational intervention demonstrated promising effects in changing these patterns, but self-care needs to be further elaborated to address the specific challenges associated with acute adjustment as well as with long-term stressors.*

Gregory C. Tomasulo and John R. McNamara (2007) The Relationship of Abuse to Women's Health Status and Health Habits - The present study examined the relationship between exposure to abuse and women's health status and health behaviors in a sample of rural women. One hundred forty-eight women visiting a community health care center completed survey packets that included measures that assessed: exposure to abuse, impairment associated with exposure to abuse, physical and mental health problems, health behaviors, and the extent of health care usage. Results indicated that exposure to abuse was positively and significantly related to the adoption of a negative psychological perspective, which in turn was negatively correlated with physical and mental health, as well as with the practice of healthy behaviors. Results also showed that women exposed to abuse engage in less healthy behaviors and utilize more health care resources than do women with no such exposure. Implications for improving the assessment and treatment of abuse in health care settings are discussed.

A. Goswami and D. Mazumder (2008) Development of Cognitive Index to Measure Health Status - One hundred ninety items were initially constructed following the prescribed guidelines to develop the cognitive index for measuring health status with the help of Equal Appearing Internal Scales described by Thurstone (1928). The scores obtained from 40 judges out of 110 were computed and subjected to item analysis comprising of calculation of median and interquartile range. One statement for each of the eleven median values was selected. In the final selection, the index consisted of 22 items with smallest interquartile range within each value. The reliability of the health status index was tested by split-half and test-retest method. The co-efficient of correlation values were 0.93 and 0.93 respectively which were found to be significant at 1 percent level of significance. It was found that the health status index constructed was highly stable and dependable for measurement.

Unna N. Danner, Henk Aarts, Esther K. Papies, Nanne K. de Vries (2009) Paving the path for habit change: Cognitive shielding of intentions against habit intrusion. The objective of the current study was to examine the cognitive processes that make it possible to use intentions to change one's habitual health-related behaviour. The study used an idiosyncratic approach to investigate personal existing habits and non-habitual behaviours in a within-participants experiment. Participants first generated habitual and non-habitual behaviours for various daily-life goals (e.g., having lunch, playing sports). Next, they formed intentions to perform non-habitual behaviours in order to attain these goals. Finally, we measured the cognitive accessibility of participants' habitual and non-habitual behaviours with a behaviour recognition task. The findings showed that habitual behaviours were more accessible than the non-habitual behaviours when no intentions were formed (control goals), showing that habits are more readily accessed in mind. However, when participants had formed intentions to use non-habitual behaviours, habitual behaviours for the same goals were inhibited in mind. This could be the cognitive mechanism that shields intentions from habit intrusion and thus enables the pursuit of non-habitual behaviours. The current study demonstrates the role of inhibitory processes in shielding non-habitual intentions in memory. These findings are discussed in the context of success and failure in changing health-related habits.

Debra Umberson, Jennifer Karas Montez (2010) Social Relationships and Health a Flashpoint for Health Policy. Social relationships—both quantity and quality—affect mental health, health behavior, physical health, and mortality risk. Sociologists have played a central role in establishing the link between social relationships and health outcomes, identifying explanations for this link, and discovering social variation (e.g., by gender and race) at the population level. Studies show that social relationships have short- and long-term effects on health, for better and for worse, and that these effects emerge in childhood and cascade throughout life to foster cumulative advantage or disadvantage in health. This article describes key research themes in the study of social relationships and health, and it highlights policy implications suggested by this research.

ANALOGY

Out of the fifteen studies to design the present investigation, the investigator has reviewed eight abroad studies from the above seven Indian studies majority of the studies belonged to survey studies and few of them are experimental studies.

Most of the studies followed Random sampling techniques for the collection of data and the size of the selected sample range from 54 to 20,776 samples. In majority studies data was collected from the Health science center in Japan and few were collected from the factory workers, military with civilian, children and undergraduate students.

In majority of the studies the questionnaire, opionnarries, adjustment tools split – half and test – retest method and rating scale developed by the investigators was utilized as a tool. Since all the reviewed studies were related to high awareness and attitude.

Mean, standard deviation and 't' test were the statistical technique followed in the majority of the studies.

The findings of the studies reported in the review of Ball Susam and Bax (2003) the results are suggested as need significant changes in Health Habits for medical students, and from finding of Gregory.C (2007) womens have less Healthy behaviors.

3

Methodology

INTRODUCTION

The main objective of the study was to find out the health habits of high schools students. The need for the study and objectives of the study were split out in chapter. I am extensive review of related literature covering the health habits and high schools students and some other related fields were presented in chapter – III. This chapter deals with the design and procedure adopted for the present study. In the simplest way research design and procedure adopted for the present study. In the simplest way research design is a plan structure and strategy of investigation in order to obtain answer to the research question. "Design is the blue print of the procedure that reaching valid conclusion about relationship between independent and dependent variables" says Best (1978). Hence to right towards the goal, it is necessary to have a design for the research being carried out at the very beginning. But it is also true that "selection of a particular design" as Best (1978) suggests, "is based on the purpose of the experiment, the types of valuables to be manipulated and the conditions or limiting factors under which it may be conducted" so it is apparent that the designs differ, as the problems differ.

The ultimate aim of such a science is to provide knowledge that will permit the educator to achieve his goals by the most effective methods.

"Scientific problems can be resolved only on the basis of data and the major responsibility of the scientist is to set up a research design capable of providing the data necessary to the solution of the problem" observed by George J Mouly (1964). The selection of methods for research work depends upon the nature of the problem selected. Mainly methodology consists of tools, techniques and procedures. The success of investigation depends on the priority of the method and the tools and techniques the researcher uses.

Research methodology is a way to solve the research problem systematically. It is necessary for the researcher to know not only the research methods and techniques but also the methodology. The methodology varies from problem to problem. The research has to specify very clearly what decisions were selected and why he did select them and low they can be evaluated by others. The purpose of study may vary from researcher to researcher. But in any form of research, the investigator has to follow certain methods. George J Mouly has classified research methods into three base types namely,

1) Historical or documentary Method
2) Experimental Method
3) Normative Survey Method

STATEMENT OF THE PROBLEM

The present study is entitled "*AWARENESS ON HEALTH HABITS AMONG HIGH SCHOOL STUDENTS IN PENNAKARAM BLOCK*"

OBJECTIVES OF THE STUDY

1. To find out the level of awareness on Health Habits among high school students.

2. To find out the level of significant difference on the awareness of Health Habits between boys and girls high school students.
3. To find out the level of significant difference on the awareness of Health Habits between hosteller's and day scholars high school students.
4. To find out the level of significant difference on the awareness of Health Habits between government and matriculation schools.
5. To find out the level of significant difference on the awareness of Health Habits between rural and urban.
6. To find out the level of significant difference on the awareness of Health Habits between educated and uneducated parents.
7. To find out the level of significant difference on the awareness of Health Habits between the parents profession.

HYPOTHESES OF THE STUDY

1. There is no significant difference between boys and girls high school students on the awareness of Health Habits.
2. There is no significant difference between hosteller's and day scholars high school students on the awareness of Health Habits.
3. There is no significant difference between government and matriculation high school students on the awareness of Health Habits.
4. There is no significant difference between urban and rural high school students on the awareness of Health Habits.
5. There is no significant difference between educated and uneducated parents children on the awareness of Health Habits among high school students.
6. There is no significant difference on the awareness of Health Habits between the parents profession among high school students.

DESIGN OF THE RESEARCH

Research design is a plan, a structure and a strategy of investigation conceived to obtain answers to various issues in research. The object to research design is to test the research hypotheses. The research design, therefore is built in the principle of maximization of variance. A research design however is not a highly specific plan to be followed without direction. Rather, it is a series of guide post to keep right direct. Thus research designs is the process of planning a research, choosing methods and procedures that can be expected to yield meaningful and most interpretable results.

The present study belong to Normative survey Research. The variables used are Gender, Locality, types of schools, Medium and Residence, parents education among high school students. It is developed by the investigator to access the awareness on Health Habits among high schools students at pennakaram black separately, along with a personal data sheet to know the back ground of the students. In this study stratified Random Sampling Technique was followed, data were collected from 150 students of 5 schools at pennakaram black. The statistical techniques Mean, Standard Deviation and 't' test were used.

Table: 1

Schematic Representation of the Research Design

S.No.	Type	Source
1.	Nature of the Research	Normative Survey Method
2.	Tool Developed	Awareness on Health Habits Rating Scale among High School Students in Pennakaram block (HHRS)
3.	Variables	Students: 1. Gender 2. Locality 3. Types of School 4. Medium 5. Parents Education 6. Residence
4.	Sampling Technique	Stratified Random Sampling Technique
5.	Size of the Sample	Samples = 150 Boys=83, Girls =67
6.	Statistical Techniques	Mean, Standard Deviation and 't' test

METHOD OF THE STUDY

In order to realize the aforesaid objectives, the normative survey method is employed. Normative survey method studies describe and interpret what exists at present. They are concerned with exists at present. They are concerned with existing conditions or relations, health habits etc., such investigations are termed in research literature as descriptive survey as normative survey.

SAMPLING

A sample is a small portion of a population selected for observation and analysis. It is a part of the subset of the whole group. It is a representative of the population which will have all the characteristics of the population.

Sampling is the process of selecting a sample from the population. Samples are not selected haphazardly, they are chosen in a systematically random way. So that chance or the operation of probability can be utilized.

"A good sample of a population is the one which will produce the characteristic of the population with great accuracy" by **Corwell (1960).** By considering what is the normal or typical condition or practice at the present time **"Sukhia et al (1969)".**

There are certain well-accepted methods often adopted for the selection of good samples. They are,

- o Random sampling
- o Stratified sampling
- o Systematic Random sampling
- o Cluster sampling

SAMPLE OF THE STUDY

For the present study is stratified random sampling method was used. This method of sampling is used when the population is composed of diverse segments or natural subdivisions of units. The method consists a classifying the population units in to a certain number of groups called strata (plural) and then selecting random samples independently from each group or stratum (singular). The division of the population into strata (termed stratification) is usually done in such a way that.

i) There is greater homogeneity within each stratum. Lesser is the variability with each stratum of the population. Greater is efficiency.
ii) There is no over-lapping in various strata
iii) As marked are the difference or possible between the various data.

For this study while selecting the sample following categories of all students studying at high school level in Pennakaram block were taken in the consideration.

SELECTION OF THE SAMPLE

The sample was selected stratified randomly representation 150 students from different school of Pennakaram block. A total number of 150 students comprising 83 male and 67 female were drawn from the following school as shown in Table:3.2

Table:2

School wise distribution of the Sample

S.No.	Sample			
	Name of the school	**Boys**	**Girls**	**Total**
1	Thiyaki Subramaniya Siva Government Boys higher secondary school, Pauparapatti.	30	_	30
2	Government girls higher secondary school, pauparapatti.	_	30	30
3	Yesuraja Matriculation high school, Pauparapatti.	23	17	40
4	Panjoyyathu union middle school, Makkanur	30	20	50
	Total	83	67	150

DETAILS OF THE SAMPLES

In this study a total member of 150 high schools students all level in pennakaram block were taken as samples. The samples are categorized in the following table.

Table: 3

Distribution of the Sample Details

S. No.	VARIABLE	SUB-VARIABLES	SAMPLE	PERCENTAGE	TOTAL
1.	Gender	Boys	83	55%	150
		Girls	67	45%	
2.	Types of School	Government	110	73%	150
		Matriculation	40	27%	
3.	Locality	Rural	69	46%	150
		Urban	81	54%	
4.	Residency	Dayscholar	112	75%	150
		Hostel	38	25%	
5.	Medium of Instruction	Tamil	110	73%	150
		English	40	27%	

METHOD OF SUMMATED RATING

The summated ratings series of items to which the subject is asked to react. The type of summated scale most frequently used in the study of health habits followed the pattern devised by Likert and referred to as Likert types of scale. In the scale the respondent indicates his several of agreement or disagreement with each item that constitutes the scale instead of indicating his agreement only for a few items. Each response is given numerical scores assigned to the entire separate item giving the total score, which is interpreted as favorable and unfavorable answer. For favorable statement the scoring order is 4,3,2,1 for the unfavorable statement scoring order is 1,2,3,4. The total score is 200 then the score is converted to 100 and analyzed are done.

Likert techniques

A method of scaling know as summate rating that is known as Likert techniques named after Likert is a widely used technique for developing an health habits scale.

The investigator assumed a large number of items relevant to the health habits scale as favorable and unfavorable. This was administrated to subjects; the subjects gave their response to each item.

In this method each proposition usually called for a responded underlying of the five words such as strongly agree (SA), agree

(A), Disagree (DA), Strongly Disagree (SDA) as a basis for determine the item to be selected for the final scale. The discriminated value of each item is calculated. This is done by obtaining the difference between the average scores for each item when the total scores are arranged in qualities.

For the present study initial hundred statements were constructed for the pilot study. After careful examination of the critical ratio for each item, it was decided to have fifty statements for the final study.

tool used for the study

The instruments employed for collecting data are called tools. "tools employ distinctive ways of describing and qualifying the data" **Best (1992).**

The tools of research are instruments that provide for the collection of data upon which, hypotheses may be tested. There are large number of tools and techniques available for data collection in research, from these tools, the researcher selects the most appropriate forms of information that could be most useful. The important tools of educational research should include schedules, questionnaire, opinionnaire, observation, checklist, rating scale, interview psychological tests and pentagrams.

By the evaluation of the different data gathering devices used in educational research the investigator was fully convinced that the development of an attitude scale will help in collecting data.

Table:4

Distribution of Positive and Negative statements of awareness on Health Habits

S.No.	Students		Total	
	Positive Items	Negative Items	Positive Items	Negative Items
1.	1,2,3,4,5,6,9,13,14,15,16,18, 20,24,25,26,29,31,33,34,35, 36,37,38,39,40,43,44,49,50	7,8,10,11,12,17,19,21, 22,23,27,28,30,32, 41,42,45,46,47,48	30	20
Total	30	20	50	

The above table 4 shows the students opionnaire to access the awareness in Health Habits among high schools students at pennakaram block. This tool HHRS consists of four point scale with 30 positive and 20 negative statements.

pilot study

The investigator being a teacher education was going on to write appropriate statements selected to the rating scale of the study. Moreover she was consulted the high school students. The steps on the different issues based on the experiences of teachers 20 high school students and others aspects the investigator refine the written statements in all the Health Habits Questionnaire. For the present study initial 80 statements were constructed for the pilot study. After careful examination of the critical ratio for each item. It was decided to have 50 statements for the final study.

COLLECTION OF DATA

The investigator obtained adequate number of copies of the rating scale for the actual collection of data. The samples high schools were visited and their heads and teachers were contacted for getting permission and co-operation for the collection of data.

The rating scale was then distributed among the students. Adequate instruction were given for making the responses. Strict uniform procedures were adopted in the administration of the rating scale to high school students of different schools. The following steps were invariably followed while administrating the rating scale.

1) Distribution of the individual rating scale to each student.
2) Giving directions of how to mark the responses in the rating scale.
3) Clearing the doubts of the students and giving additional instructions were ever necessary.
4) Giving sufficient time to mark the responses.
5) Strictly enquiring the making of independent responses.
6) Collecting all distributed rating scales.

SCORING AND CONSOLIDATION OF DATA

Each response is given numerical scores assigned to all the separate items giving the total score, which is interpreted as positive and negative answer. For positive statement scoring order 4, 3, 2, 1 and negative statement scoring order is 1, 2, 3, 4 in present study. Then the score is converted to 100 and analyses are alone. The data were collected consolidated codified and used for suitable analysis. Score of the response sheets was done as per the scoring scheme described earlier. The scores were summed up separately and the total of each individual was taken.

The fifty statements in the rating scale offer the following comprehensive view. 50 x 4 = 200, 50 x 3 = 150, 50 x 2 = 100, 50 x 1 = 50. Thus the all scores would fell maximum 200 and minimum 50 scores.

Table: 5

Distribution of Marks for Statements in Tool

S.No		Scores	
	Categories of response	Positive Statement	Negative Statement
1.	Strongly agree	4	1
2.	Agree	3	2
3.	Disagree	2	3
4.	Strongly disagree	1	4

PERSONAL DATA SHEET

The personal data sheet serves to collect personal information, students were asked to write their name, education, gender, locality, types of schools, medium of instruction and residence that they studied in High Schools.

RELIABILITY OF THE TOOL

According to Carret and Henry (1972), "Reliability means the degree to which a test or tool measure something consistently". A reliable test would definitely yield consistent result if it is administered to the different groups of equal level on the result of the pilot study the investigator found that the tool was very well understood by the student.

The investigator used karl pearson's correlation coefficient / product moment correlation. To find out the relationship between the variables. The following formula was employed.

$$\gamma = \frac{N\sum XY - \sum X \sum Y}{\sqrt{\left[N\sum x^2 - \left(\sum x\right)^2 N\sum y^2 - \left(\sum y\right)^2\right]}}$$

Where,

X = sum of the X scores

Y = Sum of the Y scores

X^2 = Sum of the squared X Scores

Y^2 = Sum of the squared Y Scores

XY = Sum of the products of paired X and Y scores

N = Number of paired scores

SPLIT HALF METHOD

The investigator used split half method to find out the reliability. In this method the test is first divided into two equivalents half's the first half of the tests represents odd number items 1,3,5,7, etc., and second half of the test represents the even number items 2,4,6,8, etc., the reliability coefficient of the whole test was calculated and it was found to be 0.9234.

$$\gamma = \frac{N\left[\sum XY - \sum X \sum Y\right]}{\sqrt{\left[N\sum x^2 - \left(\sum x\right)^2 N\sum y^2 - \left(\sum y\right)^2\right]}}$$

Reliability coefficient of the whole test.

$$r_n = \frac{2r}{r+1}$$

$$r_n = \frac{2(0.9234)}{(0.9234)+1}$$

$$r_n = 0.9602$$

r = the reliability coefficient of the half test

r_n = the reliability coefficient of the whole test

VALIDITY OF THE TOOL

Henry E Garyet defines validity as "the fidelity with which is measures what is purpose to measure". A test is valid when it measures truly and accurately the ability or equality one wan to appraise. Thus the tool was stabilized by finding the content validity. The statements were constructed properly for final study by the investigator.

STATISTICAL MEASUREMENT USED IN THE STUDY

The investigator collected the data and scoring after Mean, Standard Deviation and 't' test were used for analyses the data. The values and the interpretation of the data are given in chapter – IV of the study.

The following statistical techniques were by the investigator,

- Mean
- Standard Deviation
- Test of Significance ('t' test)

A. Mean

Mean is used to measure the entire data by one value. It is obtained by adding to gather all the items and by dividing the total by the number of items.

$$\bar{X} = A + \left[\frac{\sum fd}{N}\right] \times c$$

Where,

c = Class interval

$\sum fd$ = Total of the products of each class frequency with the steps

deviation of the respective class

N = Total frequency

$\bar{X}$ = Arithmetic mean

standard deviation

The standard deviation concept was introduced by Karl Pearson in 1823. It is used to measure dispersion standard deviation is also known as root of the mean of the square deviation from arithmetic mean.

$$S.D. = \sqrt{\frac{\Sigma fd^2}{N} - \left(\frac{\Sigma fd}{N}\right)^2} \times c$$

Where,

N = No. of samples

c = class interval

d = $\frac{X-A}{C}$

x = Midpoint of the class interval

A = Assumed mean

$\sum fd$ = Total of the products of each class frequency with the steps deviation of the respective class

$$\frac{M_1 - M_2}{\sqrt{\frac{SD_1^2}{N_1}+\frac{SD_2^2}{N_2}}}$$

$\sum fd^2$ = Total of the products of each class frequency with the square deviation of the respective class.

't' test

't' test is used to find out the significance of the means of different groups of students. For example boys and girls. The hypotheses formulated are tested using relevant statistics (ie) 't' test.

The test of significance of the difference between the two means is known as 't' test. 't' is calculated by using the below formula,

Where,

M_1 and M_2 are the means of the two variables

N_1 is number of cases in first sample

N_2 is number of cases in second sample

is standard deviation of first sample

is standard deviation of second sample

CONCLUSION

This chapter deals with methodology of the present investigation as enumerated. Thus it gives brief details about selection of sample, pilot study, administration of tool in the study, data collection and statistical technique used in this study. Having described the detailed methodology of the study in the chapter analysis and interpretation of the data for the present study is next chapter.

4

Analysis of Data

INTRODUCTION

After the research design has been implemented and the data have been collected the next step in the research process is analysis. The data after collection has to be processed and analysed in accordance with the outline laid down for the purpose at the time of developing the research plan.

In the words of Kothari.C.R.(1990), "this is essential for a scientific study and for ensuring that we have all relevant data for making contemplated comparisons and analysis". The term 'analysis' refers to the computation of certain measures along with searching for patterns of relationship that exist among data groups.

ANALYSIS OF THE DATA

Analysis of data means studying the tabulated data in order to determine the internet factor or meaning. It involves breaking down existing compiled factors in to simpler part and putting parts together in new arrangement for purpose of interpretation.

According to Wolf "the discovery of order in the phenomena of values not withstanding their complexity and apparent confusion is rendered possible by the process of analysis and synthesis which are the foundation store of all scientific methods.

LEVEL OF AWARENESS ON HEALTH HABITS AMONG HIGH SCHOOLS STUDENTS

TABLE – 7

S.No	Category	N	%
1.	High school students	150	80.5 %

The above table 7 shows that the level of awareness on Health Habits among High School students is 80.5%. It is very good awareness in Health Habits.

TESTING OF HYPOTHESIS

HYPOTHESIS: 1

There is no significant difference between boys and girls high school students on the awareness of Health Habits.

TABLE – 8

Difference on the awareness of Health Habits between boys and girls of high school students.

S.No.	Gender	No. of Samples	Mean	Standard Deviation	Calculated 't' value	Table Value (0.05)	Remarks
1	Boys	83	80.80	7.10			
2	Girls	67	80.13	9.49	0.4796	1.98	NS

From the above table 8, shows calculated 't' value is less than the tabulated 't' value at 0.05 level of significance. So the null hypothesis is accepted. So there is no significant difference between boys and girls high school students on the awareness of Health Habits. The following figure 4.1 shows the mean value of boys and girls Health Habits.

HYPOTHESIS: 2

There is no significant difference between hosteller's and day scholars high school students on the awareness of Health Habits.

TABLE -9

Difference on the awareness of Health Habits between hosteller's and dayscollers of high school students.

S.No.	Residence	No. of Samples	Mean	Standard Deviation	Calculated 't' value	Table Value (0.05)	Remarks
1	Dayscholars	112	80.4	7.19	0.06	1.98	NS
2	Hostellers	38	80.5	9.10			

From the above table 9, shows calculated 't' value is less than the tabulated 't' value at 0.05 level of significance. So the null hypothesis is accepted. So there is no significant difference between hosteller's and day scholars high school students on the awareness of Health Habits. The following figure 4.2 shows the mean value of hosteller's and dayscollers Health Habits.

HYPOTHESIS: 3

There is no significant difference between government and matriculation high school students on the awareness of Health Habits.

TABLE -10

Difference on the awareness of Health Habits between Government and Matriculation of high school students.

S.No.	Type of School	No. of Samples	Mean	Standard Deviation	Calculated 't' value	Table Value (0.05)	Remarks
1	Government	110	79.05	13.2	3.04	1.98	S
2	Matriculation	40	84.00	6.6			

From the above table 10, shows calculated 't' value is greater than the tabulated 't' value at 0.05 level of significance. So the null hypothesis is rejected. So there is significant difference between government and matriculation high school students on the awareness of Health Habits. The following figure 4.3 shows the mean value of government and matriculation Health Habits.

HYPOTHESIS: 4

There is no significant difference between urban and rural high school students on the awareness of Health Habits.

TABLE - 11

Difference on the awareness on Health Habits between urban and rural of high school students.

S.No.	Locality	No. of Samples	Mean	Standard Deviation	Calculated 't' value	Table Value (0.05)	Remarks
1	Urban	81	80.19	12.6			
2	Rural	69	80.43	6.70	0.15	1.98	NS

From the above table 11, shows calculated 't' value is less than the tabulated 't' value at 0.05 level of significance. So the null hypothesis is accepted. So there is no significant difference between urban and rural high school students on the awareness of Health Habits.

HYPOTHESIS: 5

There is no significant difference between educated and uneducated parents children on the awareness of Health Habits among high school students.

TABLE -12

Difference on the awareness of Health Habits between educated and uneducated parents among high school students

S.No.	Parents Education	No. of Samples	Mean	Standard Deviation	Calculated 't' value	Table Value (0.05)	Remarks
1	Educated	86	79.92	8.72	0.44	1.98	NS
2	Uneducated	64	80.50	7.50			

From the above table 12, shows that the calculated 't' value is less than the tabulated 't' value at 0.05 level of significance. So the null hypothesis is accepted. So there is no significant difference between educated and uneducated parents children on the awareness of Health Habits among high school students.

HYPOTHESIS: 6

There is no significant difference on the awareness of Health Habits between the parents profession among high school students.

TABLE -13

Difference on the awareness of Health Habits among high school students between cooli and Government professional of parent's.

S.No.	Parents Education	No. of Samples	Mean	Standard Deviation	Calculated 't' value	Table Value (0.05)	Remarks
1	cooli	74	79.28	8.00	1.46	1.98	NS
2	Government	44	81.41	7.50			

From the above table 13 shows calculated 't' value is less than the tabulated 't' value at 0.05 level of significance. So the null hypothesis is accepted. So there is no significant difference on the awareness of Health Habits between the parents profession among high school students.

TABLE - 14

Difference on the awareness on Health Habits among high school students between Government and private professional of parent's.

S.No.	Parents Education	No. of Samples	Mean	Standard Deviation	Calculated 't' value	Table Value (0.05)	Remarks
1	Private	33	82.47	10.00	0.51	1.98	NS
2	Government	44	81.41	7.50			

From the above table 14, shows calculated 't' value is less than the tabulated 't' value at 0.05 level of significance. So the null hypothesis is accepted. So there is no significant difference on the awareness of Health Habits between the parents profession among high school students.

TABLE – 15

Difference on the awareness on Health Habits among high school students between cooli and Private professional of parent's.

S.No.	Parents Profession	No. of Samples	Mean	Standard Deviation	Calculated 't' value	Table Value (0.05)	Remarks
1	cooli	74	79.28	8.00	1.62	1.98	NS
2	Private	33	82.47	10.00			

From the above table 15, shows calculated 't' value is less than the tabulated 't' value at 0.05 level of significance. So the null hypothesis is accepted. So there is no significant difference on the awareness of Health Habits between the parents profession among high school students.

CONCLUSION

From the above tables and figures high school students awareness on Health Habits are analyzed well. From this tables Investigator conclude frame findings. The ensuing chapter deals the findings and conclusions of the present study.

5

Findings and Conclusion

INTRODUCTION

This section is indented to provide the reader a quick review of what has been done to get the results. This portion of report is probably the most utilized part of the report. This chapter commences with the statement of problem and brief description of the procedures followed by the findings and conclusion. The recommendations of the study are also presented. Also suggestions for new studies are given.

STATEMENT OF THE PROBLEM

The present study is entitled *"AWARENESS ON HEALTH HABITS AMONG HIGH SCHOOL STUDENTS IN PENNAKARAM BLOCK"*

OBJECTIVES OF THE STUDY

1. To find out the level of awareness on Health Habits among high school students.
2. To find out the level of significant difference on the awareness of Health Habits between boys and girls high school students.

3. To find out the level of significant difference on the awareness of Health Habits between hosteller's and day scholars high school students.
4. To find out the level of significant difference on the awareness of Health Habits between government and matriculation schools.
5. To find out the level of significant difference on the awareness of Health Habits between rural and urban.
6. To find out the level of significant difference on the awareness of Health Habits between educated and uneducated parents.
7. To find out the level of significant difference on the awareness of Health Habits between the parents profession.

HYPOTHESES OF THE STUDY

1 There is no significant difference between boys and girls high school students on the awareness of Health Habits.

2 There is no significant difference between hosteller's and day scholars high school students on the awareness of Health Habits.

3 There is no significant difference between government and matriculation high school students on the awareness of Health Habits.

4 There is no significant difference between urban and rural high school students on the awareness of Health Habits.

5 There is no significant difference between educated and uneducated parents children on the awareness of Health Habits among high school students.

6 There is no significant difference on the awareness of Health Habits between the parents profession among high school students.

MAJOR FINDINGS OF THE STUDY

- There is no significant difference between boys and girls high school students on the awareness of Health Habits.
- There is no significant difference between hosteller's and day scholars high school students on the awareness of Health Habits.

- o There is significant difference between government and matriculation high school students on the awareness of Health Habits.
- o There is no significant difference between urban and rural high school students on the awareness of Health Habits.
- o There is no significant difference between educated and uneducated parents children on the awareness of Health Habits among high school students.
- o There is no significant difference on the awareness of Health Habits between the parents profession among high school students.

EDUCATIONAL IMPLICATIONS OF THE STUDY

1. More measures are to be taken at rural and urban schools to create Health Habits awareness.
2. More Programmes related to Health Habits awareness are to be conducted to the students.
3. The students may be trained to give some activities like quiz, debate, discussion, seminar, workshop etc., on Health Habits awareness.
4. Teacher may be trained to teach their lesson linked with Health Habits.
5. Government should introduce and enrich awareness on Health Habits programmes.
6. The Government has to modify the syllabus according to the needs and mental level of students.

DISCUSSION

From the findings of the present study the investigator found that 80% of the high school students have high awareness on Health Habits. This may be due to the awareness on Health Habits is good enough in all most all the areas of the Pennakaram block due to their educational status, Occupational status, Cleanliness, Role of the teachers, etc., Elders in the family provide medicines for the immediate cure on the critical illness of the people. This may make the students gain little bit of knowledge about of Health Habits.

There is no significance difference between boys and girls about the awareness of Health Habits because everyone is reading books, consulting the doctors and most of them are in joint families. There is no significance difference between hostellers and day scholars about the awareness of Health Habits because both of them having all the facilities in home as well as in hostels.

There is significant difference between government and matriculation high school students on the awareness of Health Habits. Then the private high school students have more discipline live food habits. Regulation of school activity, self discipline it implies in their daily life activity, all these disciplinary activities are lagging in government school students, hence government school students have their economic status, cleanliness home environment all these factors affect the Health Habits of government school students.

There is no significant difference between urban and rural high school students on the awareness of health habits because government is increasing the awareness of health habits by making dramas, providing hospital and toilet facilities. There is no significant difference between educated and uneducated parents children on the awareness of health habits among high school students because educated parents and uneducated parents also providing health foods basic to their children. There is no significant difference on the awareness of health habits between the parents profession among high school students because everyone feels their child health is very important comparing to others.

DISCUSSION RELATED WITH REVIEW

Based on the research contact, the findings obtained by researchers Health Habits in school students at a moderate level.

The finding of Gregory (2007) said womens are having less healthy behavior. But in this research were no significant difference from boys and girls. So it is contradichary one in the findings.

Other findings like, no significant difference from locality, parents educations and profession are newly reviewed forms this study only.

The finding like, this is significant different forms government and matriculation school student is also new finding, which is derived from this study.

So, the awareness on Health habits among high students is the new kind and new area of research.

SUGGESTIONS FOR THE FURTHER RESEARCH

The investigator would like to suggest the following for further researches.

- A comparative study on the awareness of Health Habits among the students of different categories like Elementary, Higher Secondary Students.
- A critical study on evolving strategies for promoting the awareness of Health Habits among the Arts and Science students.
- A study on the modern techniques to develop the awareness of Health Habits among the B.Ed., trainee students.
- Development of CAI package on the awareness of Health Habits.
- A study on the modern techniques to develop the awareness of Health Habits among the D.T.Ed., trainees students.

CONCLUSION

The present study made for Awareness on Health Habits among high school students. The findings of the present study reveal that the high school students having good Health Habits and high awareness. This can be analysed with the help of the variable they are Gender, Locality, Residence, Types of Schools and Medium with respect to the questionnaire. In this Matriculation student have high awareness towards the Health Habits than the Government School students, because they had knowledge towards their habits this can be elicited by the Matriculation School teachers with help of many awareness programme.

Index